MARRY HIM

AND

Be Submissive

MARRY HIM
AND
Be Submissive

COSTANZA MIRIANO

TAN Books
Charlotte, North Carolina

CONTENTS

A Note from the Publisher

In November of 2013, a book was published that caused an uproar among feminists all over Europe. You now hold that book in your hands.

Costanza Miriano's *Casate y se sumisa* (*Get Married and Be Submissive*) created shockwaves as it became a bestseller and climbed the charts of European Amazon rankings. But with the widespread circulation of Miriano's book, and an endorsement from *L'osservatore Romano* (the daily newspaper of the Vatican), came criticism from feminist groups who staged protests from Italy to Spain, where they ripped up copies in the streets and demanded a ban on the book, claiming it promoted "violence against women."

Despite the outrage from some, the book is popular for a reason. Its title comes from St. Paul's Letter to the Ephesians, and it brings Christian teachings on marriage, from St. Paul to St. John Paul II, to a contemporary audience in a winning way.

Perhaps never before has someone taken such sound theological teachings and dressed them up with such wit and humor. On one page, Miriano will have you rolling on the ground with laughter. On the next, she will have you pausing in deep reflection at her profound insights into marriage, parenting, and the state of the world.

Marry Him and Be Submissive takes the form of a series of letters to Miriano's friends and family. In these letters, she forces her readers to ponder the reasons behind the moral decay of our civilization and the crumbling of family life. She tackles a minefield of contemporary issues, including the differences between men and women; the difficulty of raising daughters in a sex-crazed culture; young people delaying marriage and children; weak fathers who fail to fulfill their proper role; the tragedy of abortion and the harmful effects of the contraceptive culture; and the many challenges that arise for working moms. She tackles these serious subjects with an endearing charm that plays off her life experiences as a mother of four children who just so happens to be a successful Italian journalist as well.

Mothers of young children will appreciate the humorous spin Miriano gives to the chaos that comes with raising kids and will find encouragement in handling the many (sometimes overwhelming!) demands of their state of life. But this book is not just for mothers, or even just for women. Miriano's insights will strike a chord with women and men alike. She uses hilarious candor to point out the differences between husbands and wives and shows how these very differences make the bond of marriage stronger when handled in the proper way—with charity and humility.

The feminists who took to the streets in protest may never see the true value of this groundbreaking book, but their outrage is misguided. Miriano has accomplished what feminists have been trying to do for decades. She has given women a roadmap to true liberation, not from men or an oppressive culture, but from the pitfalls of original sin and an unfulfilling life of chasing the false promises of this world.

Since this edition is a translation from Italian, the reader may find the occasional unfamiliar slogan or expression and will find many more references to soccer than to football. But Miriano's depictions of the struggles and joys of human life, especially those found in marriage and in the family, are universal. It is our hope that this book will help you overcome those struggles and enliven those joys so that you will find strength and peace amidst a world that wants so badly to destroy the Christian family. We hope also that it will make you howl with laughter; something tells us it will do all these things and more.

INTRODUCTION

LOOK WHO'S TALKING!

"Costanza, tell me again why I should go ahead and get married in two weeks?"

I reach for the cell phone earpiece. I put the soft drink can away in the holder—thank God for American cars. I need to spit out the mandarin orange seeds. (Dear husband, I promise that one day soon, I'll bring a plastic bag and tidy up all my Pocket Coffee wrappers!) I'm going to have to clean out this pigsty that passes for a car—the car of a dissolute woman who snacks at traffic lights along the banks of the River Tiber. Right now, I need to turn it into a counselling room—instantly—a kind of poor woman's Oprah Winfrey studio.

The great thing about friendship isn't so much having someone close to you who tells you things straight to your face . . . things like how that "rotten onion" shade of highlights you've just put in your hair doesn't show off your new bob to the best effect. Or someone who will try really hard to find a good reason you should buy yourself a ninth black stone necklace because, if you only had that necklace, it would solve all your wardrobe problems. Or someone who will tell you what a fantastic plan

1

you had, how you carried it out to perfection, and how it wasn't really your fault that the 14 little friends your children invited over to your house managed to escape your attention for a second and kick a ball that wrecked the only two rose bushes that had ever flowered . . .

No. From my point of view, having good friends is essential for another reason: It allows me to give out advice—an activity that I find hugely gratifying.

The fact is that friends—female friends, to be more precise— tend to come into contact with me for a short time and therefore can put up with a quite intense burst of advice from me.

Children, on the other hand, to whom I cling like a limpet, seem to be able to turn the sound right down to "off" when I start my little sermons. And they look at me, focusing their gaze on one of my earrings while they think about the latest *X-Men* adventure, which they will be able to continue reading when I shut up about the benefits of a methodical and accurate study plan.

As for my husband, he is an intelligent man and has learned to reply instantly, "Right" or "Really?" or "Indeed" or even "Absolutely, I agree" (and almost always with just the right tone of voice). This is a skill that allows him to pretend to be in conversation with me while costing him the minimum of effort. If I have any doubts that he is not listening to me, I test him by saying something like "Darling, I'm pregnant again," at which point he lets out a noise like someone being strangled, and this proves that somehow at least the superficial extremes of what I am saying are getting through to him.

My female friends, however, seem to listen to my opinions and, in fact, occasionally take them seriously. Perhaps they do so more out of affection than through any great belief that my psychological insights (which are those of a rampaging center back) have any real chance of being accurate. Though—let's be honest—I must be right occasionally, as a matter of statistical probability, if nothing else.

Normally, my response to any problem is one of the following: "He's right"; "Why not have a baby?"; "Just do what he says"; "Have you thought of having another baby?"; "You should move to his home city"; "Try to forgive him"; "Try to understand him"; or again, "Have a baby!"

For this reason, those friends of mine who don't want to hear such advice—and I know that I can be as delicate as a bull in a china shop if I really try—disappear off my radar. I am quite on the ball about things, and normally after having sent them 13 e-mails without reply or after having received 4 extremely short responses to my texts, I get the message.

Those who think the way I do, however, or those who, despite everything, still like me, continue to call. That gives me great satisfaction.

The reason, dear husband, that you so often hear the phrase "Give me a second. I am just going to say hello to my friend. I'll be right with you" is that, as I have said, giving out advice is fantastic. Besides, there is no better way to pretend that I have something important to do when all hell is breaking loose—like when the two boys are bashing each other with water bottles from their bikes in a fight over the quarter-inch-high head of a LEGO man, which has a mustache and neither of them can live without, while at the same time my two daughters have knocked over a box of tiny pasta shapes that are now scattered all over the floor.

But more than anything else, my female friends and I need each other because we do not have, unlike women of previous generations, a clear life path laid out for us.

Sometimes we find ourselves thinking aloud, discussing our ideas about life, identity, and options, which are many—indeed, more than ever in recent years. That's why we have to call each other. At this juncture in history, more than ever before, it is important—indispensable, even—to spend a stratospheric amount of money on phone bills (the phrase "I'll stop by your house," at least in Rome, is a nonstarter).

Our lives are made up of our own personal balancing acts that are so unique to ourselves that we can feel quite lonely sometimes. We need to find a new way of being a couple at a period in history when, for a while, there hasn't been a standard shared vision of how that life as a couple should be lived out. (I have taken part in lengthy discussions among couples about, for example, the weekly dinner menu, and I have looked back with painful nostalgia to those days when husbands would peek through the kitchen door at meal times to ask, "What's for dinner?" Less sharing, perhaps, but a lot less complicated!)

Nowadays, we need to find time for work, family, our spouses, and even, theoretically, if we ever manage it, ourselves.

The truth is that no woman that I know is obsessed with the same problems that certain feminists and endless newspaper articles seem to think are important. All those advertisements about the female body, seen as an object of beauty; all the issues about the cruel rules of success and the image-conscious society that wants us to be forever young and that obliges us, poor things, to opt for plastic surgery; all the issues surrounding the need to win back our autonomy—these bother us very little when we are in line at the supermarket on a rainy day and we have to deal with picking up one son from soccer, the other from catechism classes, while one daughter is sleeping and the other has to go to the bathroom!

Maybe I have chosen an unusual circle of friends, but none of us consider our freedom to be seriously threatened. None of us feel that when we begin a relationship, we are oppressed or troubled by the position of the pope on the issue. It just doesn't arise! None of us feel that our freedom to manage our fertility has ever been suffocated by some pronouncement of "the Church that likes to say no," which seems to bother the newspapers so much. Indeed, it seems that speaking badly about the Church is *the new black*: It goes well with everything and never goes out of fashion!

None of my friends are upset because they have been unable to have an abortion in the comfort of their own home, but many are burdened because they have been unable to have a child, maybe through age, maybe because of a scared partner, or maybe because their lives are so complicated that they cannot begin to think about it.

I know many women who are anxious about short-term contracts and the instability of a working life that makes it almost impossible to make long-term plans.

We are annoyed and bothered, greatly bothered even, by the hostility that the world of work shows toward our children. It would appear that only by putting them in an orphanage can we hope to reach the same professional level as those colleagues who don't have any children. We even have to be careful not to speak about them too much in the office. We may be allowed a photo of the kids at the bottom of the second desk drawer, under a copy of *Vanity Fair*—that may be just about allowable.

We normal women get bothered at times when one of the children has a 102-degree temperature on the very week that their grandparents are off on vacation—it is a scientific fact that these things happen at the same time—and the babysitter cannot come because she has the same virus as the child. And of course, all this happens when Dad's work commitments cannot be altered. In such cases, a mother who stays at home with the child and doesn't take a sick day so as not to tell a lie (something that we are not supposed to do—I've been pretty sure of that since my first year of catechism classes) finds herself facing one of the following options: having her pay docked; having her pension rights affected; or having to sign an affidavit—whatever that is—before a council official, which will mean taking a day of annual leave anyway!

And all of this at a period when children are supposed to be the future of society. That annoys us!

We get annoyed about films for children that are full of double entendres and nods and winks to the grown-ups, which mean we cannot just say to the kids, "Go and watch a bit of television, darling," because although it seems OK sometimes to use the television as an electronic babysitter, the Good Mother in us, alas, is always vigilant.

It is she, the Good Mother, who obliges us, for example, to say calmly, "Darling, perhaps it would be better if you don't throw yourself head-first off the bunk beds wearing my best evening dress as Batman's cape." Because this time the Good Mother is going to be calm, take charge of the situation, and avoid shouting.

And it is that Good Mother that I *should* be who obliges me to paint on a sweet smile when I get up in the morning after working late, after just four hours sleep, and find myself having to sort out an argument that was left hanging from the night before. At such times, in truth, I feel as though I need to dedicate all my energy to remember which contact lens should go in my right eye, which if I am not mistaken is the same side as the hand I use to write. (Early in the morning, some skills should not be required in a civilized country . . .)

These are our daily problems. Not the glass ceiling, not that barrier that, according to the feminists, is transparent but impenetrable and that prevents us taking our place at the top table.

These days there are new forms of couples to define, since the roles that we have had from the beginning are continually up for discussion. It is worse than the government's agreement with steelworkers——at least that lasts a couple of years!

Nowadays, families are unstable. Now that fertility has become manageable, this has had an enormous—and, to some extent, still unexplored—impact on the lives of women who can, if they wish, decide on questions like when and how often to give the gift of life. Although the unexpected can also happen, as nature doesn't allow itself to be manipulated without a cost.

Nowadays, women have many more options open to them; they almost always work, and therefore the division of labor—and even identity—is "liquid," to use a fashionable word.

So we end up discussing these issues, searching for some sort of common ground.

Discussion goes on among friends and even acquaintances, since we only need an hour at a children's party to share our intimate insights amid the bits of squashed pizza and rivers of pear juice. When we get together even for an aperitif with some nice cheeses and dips, and even when there is no children's talent show blaring out of the television in the background, the same questions arise.

And I think that we all come up with the same answers—it's just that I don't know why we seem to be in a hurry to forget about them and forget that when we distort our nature, we become unhappy and anxious.

Think about it: We can win something in the lottery almost every day; we live in the right time in the right part of the world where we can read what we want and where books and the Internet are easily available; we can go out for a run without fear of getting shot; we can go into a church and light a candle in front of a Pinturicchio masterpiece because we don't live in those parts of the world where the oldest work of art dates back to 1902 or where they would cut our throats because we have a Bible in the house. We can eat more or less what we want, and our parents, even though they are not so old themselves, will tell us about how they longed for a spoonful of sugar or about how they used to rub salami on their bread so that when they went back to eat it later, there was a lingering taste . . .

For these and for many other reasons, we should really be jumping for joy when we put a foot out of the bed in the morning. The fact that we don't is because there is a mysterious deep hunger inside us that is never fully satisfied and also because we have forgotten why we are here.

Women are called to collaborate in giving life in every way possible: by giving birth and supporting, listening to, and encouraging their children and the children of others.

Our genius is in forging relationships more than anything else. That seems obvious to me. If you want proof, think what the social life of the family would be like if it were left to the men. We would be wandering around the streets without saying hello to a living soul, or so it seems, since every time you say a few words to someone (the neighbor, the pediatrician, the catechist), the man at your side will ask, "Who was that?" and "How on earth do you know all these people?"

Only we women know how to find the right language and translate it, even though at times we need an interpreter for those closest to us. (When my husband, for example, says, "Of course, darling," what he really means is, "I will do it, but it's obvious that I would much prefer not to be at our neighbor's son's First Communion party." Such an invitation is one of the worst things that can happen to him, a guy whose conviviality is such that unless some major incident occurs—such as losing his keys—he prefers not to waste words.)

We women have a special talent for welcoming, accepting, and educating—and not only with our own children. We are able to see the good in ourselves and in others. We display hope when this good seems just a little spark of faraway light. We seem to be able to see the good in situations even when we have to screw up our eyes to make it out. Even when it's a "dark and stormy night" and you would need the imagination of a master storyteller to see the bright side.

And you need infinite patience to constantly repeat the same basic requests—how we would be much happier if the kids did not put their shoes on the sofa or their fingers up their nose and then their hands on the plate. Or, in truly extreme circumstances, how we would really appreciate it if they were to use a little soap. (My eldest son came back from camping recently with his tube of body wash still sealed—clearly there had been no emergency during his week away.) If we deny this vocation to patient service, things don't add up.

We women feel the need to give life—to defend it, sustain it, and support it. Sometimes it seems to be that women of my generation, who for the first time in history have the luxury of deciding whether to accept this role or not, decide against it in haste and without due consideration. Maybe just because they can say no, they do. The trouble comes when they realize, too late, that it was not, on reflection, the right decision for them. They realize too late that a woman finds herself in giving and that when there is someone in need of protection, we find the strength to come to his or her aid, no matter how disastrous our own situation may be.

It's a powerful force, the maternal instinct, one that a certain kind of feminism has tried to deny. To those who say that there is no such thing as a natural, maternal instinct, that it can be explained away as some kind of cultural conditioning, I suggest a visit to a daycare center. There you will see arrayed rows of little soldiers, cab drivers, and builders and a line of little brides, nurses, and cooks. Can they all be children of parents who oppressed and brainwashed them?

We can be maternal toward anyone who needs help. As Origen puts it, even our prayers "are the mothers of what happens in the world." Women, when they experience motherhood—not necessarily physical motherhood—are transfigured by happiness. They seem to set aside their own problems and roll up their sleeves. Often they become hugely affectionate and generous mothers, even if before they had been crazy, full of outbursts like "Why are you looking at me?" and "Who told you about me?"

To renounce one's own desires for the sake of others' happiness is a cure for every wound, though at the moment of decision it can be a painful choice to make. Think about what it is like when you are trying to sneak out for a dangerous liaison—Philip Roth awaits you in the bookstore—and the cry is raised that one of the children has a temperature that is sky high, something you suspected, but why oh why does the confirmation have to come just as you are in the driveway ready to go out?

Many women who constantly delay, often for trivial reasons of practicality or organization, this courageous step in life—becoming mothers—suffer, often without realizing it.

And so to all of them, and to myself and those like me when we forget our priorities and why we are here, I feel the urge to loudly proclaim two or three things.

I personally heard the call to give advice in grade school when I shared with the teacher—and I must admit to anyone else remotely interested—pearls of wisdom such as "We must all try to be better." I quickly realized that it was easier said than done, that words were far more comfortable than silent, good examples. Reserve, discretion, and silent consideration are no good to me. They are too difficult, they don't give any pleasure—I mean, what if no one noticed me?

From that moment on, I embraced my vocation as a preacher with great zeal. I know that because I remember all too well the pillow fights that knocked my glasses off when I suggested to my brothers that they should switch off the cartoons and dedicate themselves more to reading and that this would contribute rather more to their development than *Tom and Jerry*. I was nine.

All of this explains why, when I got that phone call from my friend who was in the middle of a prenuptial crisis, I was ready to respond in a flash. Any counselor worthy of the name should be ready to drop everything and turn up for an emergency special, even when she is wearing a GAP skirt with Nutella fingerprints engrained so deeply that they have become part of the pattern and a top that was once white but is now that unique shade "trademark Costanza" (a washed-out shade of grey that can be achieved by getting it wrong with absolute precision for seven consecutive washes). I make a quick agenda for the talk in my head:

- I must be convincing.
- Recall the grace of the sacrament that will make all things new.
- Point out that husband-to-be Domenico is a great guy.
- Underline the fact that a little trepidation is inevitable when you are about to do something that will last your whole life, even signing up for a lifetime's free supplies from Macy's.
- Insist on the fact that if she doesn't stop living only for herself, she will bear no fruit.

- Don't mention the fact that she will want to go to sleep just as he will want to share with her some fabulous news such as the workings of his new computer. Big wow! Or try to get her to decide on bathroom tiles when her eyes are closing with tiredness. (Anyway, why do we have to make these decisions? To me it's a form of cruelty.) Every time I've moved, I've asked the salesman if he could supply a mix of tiles based on my current favorites (though I do confess that I have noticed his pained expression each time I walked into the shop). What is this convention about ordering by the square foot anyway?

Anyhow, I will find arguments to counteract this attack of panic from the bride-to-be. If the traffic lights are not all green—and that would be quite impossible in Rome—I've got at least 24 minutes of telephone conversation to avert the tragedy, even if, as I see it, a couple of seconds should be enough.

After all, Domenico knows how to toss a salad, he can play "I Can See Clearly Now" on the guitar, he's got a copy of St. Teresa of Avila's *Path of Perfection* on his bedside table, and he is even pretty good at choosing purses. What else could you want in a husband?

I don't know what else we want; we grumble discontentedly so much. Maybe we lack the courage to see our greatness, our true greatness. Maybe we don't understand that we have an enormous capacity for giving, for spending ourselves, and in doing so, resolving so many useless worries and in the process infecting our men with good without drowning them in requests.

On rereading these saintly words of St. Teresa, I fear I may have given an image of myself that is rather too benevolent—I might have come across as some kind of luminous, wise, hard-working woman who would never be found (as she is at this precise moment) nibbling at dried fruit in front of a computer screen, trying to summon up enough strength to eliminate a square yard or two from the ironing pile that is building up in the corner.

I may seem like a devoted wife, always on the ball, who from the first day of her marriage was able to set aside her own self-ishness and generously make space for her husband. (I did actu-ally leave him a drawer for his things . . .) I may come across as a patient, caring mother, able to be strong and authoritative when necessary, one who would never yell just because her pearl neck-lace got broken during a scuffle between the two little princesses and who would always know with absolute certainty how to care sweetly for her offspring. I may come across as an angel of the home rather than someone who would prefer to do anything other than cook dinner, who would read whatever is to be found in the kitchen—fascinating texts such as how to freeze puree or that fanciful instruction leaflet for the burn cream—because the truth is that any written word seems more interesting than cooking the meat.

While I absolutely forbid anyone to check the reality with my husband—that wouldn't be fair, it would be below the belt—I will spontaneously and willingly confess that the hardworking and wise woman that I would like to be, besides giving advice in abundance, asks for it in equal measure.

That's the thing about advice: It goes back and forth—for which the telephone companies are eternally grateful.

For any issues to do with health, there's my sister, an extremely able doctor who hides her light under the bushel of her real profession—that of a civil engineer. My sister really comes into her own on those occasions when I diagnose myself with some terrible illness that I can't allow myself to succumb to, at least not until my kids access the mysterious secret of how to put a dirty sock in the hamper. It would be terrible to imagine them wandering lost around the house saying to each other, "Let's read her diaries. Maybe she wrote in there how to do it."

At such times I call my sister, I describe my symptoms, and she asks me if the pain is above my pancreas. I respond, "Where is my pancreas? Don't ask me difficult questions. Just tell me that it's not serious!" Usually I'm happy to hear generic responses: "If it hurts, it's not a tumor!" And then she starts talking about the thyroid and other glands that I don't even know if I possess (could I have swallowed my thyroid?), so I move the discussion on to other topics—such as that lovely green handbag in the Miu Miu shop.

For anything to do with children's health, however, there is always my husband's sister, another highly efficient and soothing medic. Even as her son is about to take his final college exams, she remembers the right dose of aspirin (based on body weight) for my kids, because she, unlike me, knows what my children weigh and can work out the symptoms of the standard childhood illnesses. For me, unfortunately, everything medical seems new, as exciting as an unread novel, because anything to do with health issues goes in one of my ears and out the other.

On the other hand, I can still recall, years after the event, everything about Detective Peterson, a fantastic character that I made up after my son got his foot stuck in the spokes of his grandpa's bike. You, dear reader, may have applied ice, I guess. But for me, the first thing that came to mind was the urgent need to invent a story to dry his tears. (The same story was useful years later when trying to get him to eat his minestrone, because as we all know, Detective Peterson got his job in the NYPD through eating lots of vegetables.)

Then there's Emmanuela. I strongly advise you not to call her at dinnertime. Because if the conversation should inadvertently lead to you asking, "What are you making for dinner?" she will tell you how she saw the most beautiful broccoli and some fantastically fresh tilapia at the market. You, who wouldn't know what fresh tilapia looks like nor how to distinguish beautiful broccoli from ugly broccoli, will be forced to reply that now that it's eight o'clock, you will open the fridge and try to rustle up an omelet if you can find an egg that's not out of date. Sometimes you might even find in there some cannelloni left by my mother-in-law who was bringing one of the girls back from dance class.

A small digression, aimed at my mother . . . I know I ask you every time for the recipe for your bean casserole—it's just that the last time I wrote it on a paper tissue that I then duly used to clean the marble floor. The only recipe that I have managed to memorize with exact precision is the least useful for our average guest—who tends to be under 11, missing a few teeth, and sometimes has a pacifier in his or her mouth—a superhot version of goulash.

With Costanza, my namesake and school friend, we come to grips with the joys of modern life, such as birthday parties in shopping centers, the curse of children's entertainers, and the return of illiteracy among my journalist colleagues and her college students.

If I have to organize something, the queen of common sense is Chiara, a woman capable of having eight people over to dinner three days after giving birth and of preparing a six-course meal, all the while disregarding the stitches from the Caesarean section and the baby at her breast. When I look at her, I think I need a trainer in my life. If I could, I think I would choose Sepp Guardiola, who in his first year as manager of FC Barcelona won everything there is to win. (It's not that I would want him because he's extremely handsome. No, of course not.) But I don't think I could afford his salary!

With almost all my friends—with my closest friend Marina and all the others—we can pass with great agility from the highest levels of conversation (spirituality, art, literature) to the lowest levels (gossip, eyebrow shapes, impulse buying). With all of them, there's a constant openness to finding a balance in our lives and evaluating the worth of our respective existences. We can talk, even without the help of mind-altering drugs, late into the night. (This is largely because, until the kids are all in bed, we are limited to short service announcements: "Tomorrow at four o'clock at the soccer field at Testaccio . . . I'll take them, you bring them back . . . snack is in the bag.")

And in all of this, you, dear men of our lives, think that many of these phone calls are superfluous, that this week is much like the last, given that there have been no epochal changes such as the birth of a new child, a change of job, or a new set of highlights. But it's not like that! You have to keep up!

We can always improve in the art of complaining, a skill in which I personally reach outstanding levels of creativity and conviction: "I'm tired. I want to be the golf correspondent of CNN. No, I want to retire to a hermitage above the Passo del Furlo to write a book; will you look after the children for me? No, maybe I should leave my job, spend my days doing embroidery, and always be at home with the children. Do you think I could make an effective contribution to the family income given that my idea of embroidery is sewing on a button? Is there much of a market for professional button fixers?"

We lament and we listen to others' lament, and that's about it! We are female versions of that character the Italian songster Riccardo Cocciante sang about in his classic hit, "Un Nuovo Amico" (A New Friend): "If you wake him up in the night—it's already happened—he comes down in his pajamas, takes a hiding from you and gives you one in return . . ."

But enough of all that.

Now, without further ado, it's the bride's turn for some advice.

CHAPTER 1

MONICA

OR

TO INFINITY, AND BEYOND!

Dear Monica,

You ask me why you should get married? As my friend Giulia, from the perspective of a 25-year-old newly-wed, puts it, I would ask you the opposite question. How can you think of not getting married?

How can you think of going through life—the only life that you have—with a man, leaving the door a little bit open, just in case something doesn't work out or doesn't suit you? It's obvious that something won't work! A man wandering about your house—always the same one, always there in absolute control of the TV remote . . . silences that you can't explain; a guy who asks you how you are and then leaves the room when you begin to reply, who for years won't remember your friends' names but will remember that of his favorite actress, and who will never fully appreciate your genius as a film critic able to sum up the movie directly from the theater seat, whispering to him your exclusive review there and then . . .

OK, but these are details. I have heard you say wonderful things about Domenico, and I've never seen any doubt in those eyes of yours. Since you met him, those eyes have been happier than they've ever been at any time since I've known you.

You wouldn't need to be a genius to work out that you two are made for each other like one of those little wooden duck puzzles that the children have. I am never able to put the parts back together. I always seem to put the tail where the beak should be. The kids' chubby little hands seem to be better at it than mine as soon as they turn two. (Their manual dexterity on the computer surpasses mine about the age of three!)

You are his enthusiasm; he is your balance. He is the spring in your step; you are his right arm. I don't want to set myself up as a wordsmith in some local song contest, but I think you get my meaning.

It's true that he does have some little defects of course. He dresses as though he is color blind, he has an insane passion for the outdoor life, and he shows incredible enthusiasm for teaching you the mating call of the rare hoopoe bird when the only sound you really want to hear as you read on the sofa is the drone of the dishwasher.

He's a fanatic for plots and is always trying to explain to you the secret powers that control the world when you have difficulty remembering what happened yesterday.

In terms of the fundamentals, however, you two are a perfect match. And among those things that really count—loyalty, solidity, and goodness—he is just what you need.

We've spoken so often—long before you two got together, during our long years as single women—about what our Mr. Perfect would be like.

"Will I bump into him in the supermarket while I'm dressed in a horrific spandex tracksuit?" you asked yourself in anguish one day. "Or maybe," you wondered out loud, "it will be the new guy who starts in the office tomorrow." To prepare yourself, you made an array of purchases, culminating in that Givenchy sheath dress—all of which were useless. Well, maybe not totally useless, since you did put the dress on when you decided to go out with that "friend" of yours who had been in love with you forever, a friend called Domenico, whom you were to discover you loved too.

He always had a crush on you, and as everyone knows, nothing encourages a man more than playing a little hard to get, having a phone that's always busy and a door that's always closed (I never managed that trick, but stylish women know how to do it).

Among the reasons to get married, I certainly would *not* include the fact that you have already made a lot of preparations. They don't matter if you decide not to get married. Anyway, you two are taking it calmly, and getting married is more about the sacrament than what others might think. I wouldn't worry too much about the loss of income that would befall that hairdresser who had offered to create what looked to me like a variant on a white fritter on your head, making you look quite ridiculous for the princely sum of $900. Nor would I worry too much about the makeup artist who had applied that "tart" look to you.

Better, surely, a low-profile lunch at home and understated elegance. Wedding feasts are overrated (a bit like organic food being consumed in a river of smog) and almost always as loud and loutish as a vacation on the Red Sea. Therefore, don't worry about taking a step back; you can do so at very little cost, apart from a hysterical outburst from your mother who was looking forward to getting rid of you at last.

The low-key marriage that you had planned seems to me to be the foretaste of a happy life together, unlike those who celebrate "the happiest day of their lives" (says who?) as though it were a show business event. It's important to try to leave some meaning in a ceremony that for some, alas, has no real meaning at all.

It is certainly not all about the "consummation" of the first night, which is only a distant memory anyway for those who are already living together and are getting married to give their relationship what they call a "boost." God, called on to witness the whole affair, is a vague shadow in the background for them. In fact, the vague background shadow might not be present at all were it not for the fact that a church setting is a bit more romantic, more solemn, with all those candles and frescoes, which, unfortunately, are often meaningless to those in attendance.

What boost to your relationship can there be in a leather-bound photo album with photomontages of her on the palm of his hand? Or the meal for three hundred guests and the chauffeur-driven limousines rented for the day? I sometimes think that the excesses of a wedding day and the solidity of a marriage are in inverse proportion to each other.

The measured, elegant, meaningful ceremony you've planned is the prelude to the birth of a new family, I'm sure of it.

But with the big day approaching, it seems to me that a doubt or two are allowable, even obligatory. It happened to me too, despite my convictions, despite the perfect scenario for a marriage proposal, which could not have been better, not even if Nora Ephron had come up with it. There I was—minus thirteen years and four children but one dress size better off (details that would have been important to the director of casting)—in a little Italian restaurant in New York with the best spaghetti in tomato and basil sauce (no meatballs!) I had ever tried . . . but please don't tell my mom that!

But when they come, the words "Will you marry me?" always have a certain impact, even if you have been waiting for them and maybe even soliciting them through a little subtle psychological pressure ("Don't you want to say something to me by any chance?" or "Given that you do want to say something to me, why not say it now when the moment is perfect?").

When it happens, you're taken aback. Is he actually saying it? What if I'm making a mistake? And what will happen if, when we move in together, I discover that every Sunday he has some strange habit of folding his tracksuit away carefully in plastic sheets? And what if he stops making an effort with himself, emits awful noises, and even wants his own space on the bathroom shelf that I consider to be exclusively my own?

I would dismiss your doubts as the normal reaction of someone who is making a lifelong choice—an action that has become pretty much obsolete in a world that exalts doubt and all things short term as the distinctive characteristics of a free and illuminated mind.

Yet it's evident that every choice we make requires a "no" as well as a "yes." We can't escape that. Even those who think they are not choosing are, in reality, choosing one particular path and ignoring all the others.

Those who choose casual relationships are saying no to the complexity and depth of giving oneself completely without holding anything back. Those who decide for a definitive gift of self say no to much else, perhaps to carefree pleasures, certainly to independence.

You are about to say yes to Domenico. (You will say yes—it's clear to me. You certainly wouldn't want me to be going on about it for the next 15 years!) And you're about to say no to that shadowy colleague of yours who is always making eyes at you, and to all those other people of your past and your future. And you're about to say no to that freelance work in Brussels and the contract in Pisa. (As a married couple, it's best to live together, if possible.) You're saying no, too, to all the other possible ideas that still float around your head asking to be considered.

Alarm is a normal part of the process. After all, "until death do you part" could be quite a long time!

But is life really worth living if you don't build something that goes beyond yourself?

If the option is there to walk away, it will be a temptation for one of you to do so, at least every forty years or so. (For others the temptation might come more regularly—especially after the ninth consecutive hour spent watching old movies or after one too many comments about Francesco Totti's soccer skills.)

But it would be a sin, a big, extremely stupid, irreparable sin. Because in the marriage exchange, there is that total giving of self that every heart craves. There is that someone with whom you can really be yourself. Someone with whom you can feel yourself loved for who you really are. In marriage there is someone to learn to love ever more deeply and completely in a way that those who have not chosen a single person for the whole of their life can't imagine.

There is also a lot more that "I can't talk about here," as Italian singer Gino Paoli puts it. I can't go into it too precisely—I'm too modest! But believe me, a stable relationship can bring you surprises in *all* areas!

You will be happy at having waited for him to become your husband, and maybe you'll be sorry that you threw yourself away in previous relationships—paying homage to the sexual consumerism that we inhale in the air of the age in which we live. The problem is not so much that they were *premarital* relationships; it's that they were *extramarital* relationships. They weren't about the union of persons—the daily, continuous, and definitive gift of self. They could never fulfill your hopes in life.

They were pleasurable—absolutely—who can deny it? But nothing compares to the pleasure of a physical love when two people love each other with all their strength, sharing together their hardships as well as their space and time.

When you get past the stage of tiredness, it's like getting to level 2 in one of those video games and discovering new territories. It's true that wiping up neonatal vomit may not be the most exciting thing in the world, I accept that, but that stage passes. There is light at the end of the tunnel.

But there is always that old voice in our ear—it has been there since the Garden of Eden—that says that self-determination, following freely every emotion, will make us free and happy. We mustn't be like those poor repressed souls who hold out for heaven in the hope of their consolation prize.

This is simply not true. I see no shortage of people scratching away at rashes of their own making. The truth is, as Chesterton wrote, "There is nothing more transgressive and exciting than orthodoxy." Marriage is fun; it's natural and it responds to our needs and desires for happiness.

My husband would never admit it in front of eye-witnesses, but even he is happy to have married that crazy creature who forgets about the potatoes in the oven and remembers about them twenty miles into the drive, trying, even then, to find the positive side to the situation (I haven't found it yet, but there must be one, I'm sure).

My husband is deep down glad to have found me even if I do sometimes take the kids out without checking that they have underwear on, even if after years of practice, I still only know three routes through Rome and follow them constantly even when I am trying to get to a totally different district, placing blind trust in Providence that it will somehow bring me to my destination.

Marriage is a kind of scaffolding that protects those of us, men and women, who choose it. It protects us from our inconsistency; it helps us. It encourages us to find new paths when the old ones seem to all be dead ends (speaking of, I really must buy myself a GPS). It tells us who we are in relation to another person who knows everything there is to know about us, including our egos. And it is fun! Maybe I have said that before, but what do you expect from someone who forgets the potatoes in the oven? Ah, here it is, I have found it: Maybe the positive in that burnt potato scenario was that the house didn't burn down!

You can have a perfectly good married life even when you are both in bed, in silence, and you think you are in the middle of a full-blown marital crisis; when you are secretly consumed with anxiety, asking yourself how your relationship got to this stage while he stares silently at the ceiling. If he tells you that he is not thinking of anything, trust him. Believe him! He is not thinking about anything. Don't always believe that he is thinking of leaving you. If he is staring at the ceiling, chances are that he is probably thinking one of these perfectly innocent thoughts:

- Look at that hole! I will have to seal it up.
- Let's hope that there is a decent referee on Sunday.
- I'd love a beer, but I'm too lazy to get up.

It's not that your relationship is in crisis. It's just that you are different.

The rough edges that need smoothing down are many at the beginning, such as his stupid use of the potholder in the kitchen and his tendency to store rotten cucumbers and tomatoes in the fridge. And the way in which he will leave bits of clothing in unlikely places may seem to you almost inconceivable. Certainly incomprehensible is his ability to change the channel just when the kiss is about to happen, and incredible is his stubbornness in forgetting the most important thing on the shopping list, that very item you need to make the dinner. The wall separating his sleeping and waking states will be impenetrable at night when the children cry. Extraordinary will be his ability to be away for work when the kids come down with some infection, and the farther he is away, the more frequently the coughing fits will occur. Unforeseeable will be his decree that it's time to let fresh air into the bedrooms, despite the fact that it's below zero outside and you are trying to get your children into their thick pajamas. Inexplicable will be his inability to do more than one thing at once, and I am not talking about reading a philosophical treatise while playing the violin; I just mean the ability to talk and heat a baby's bottle at the same time.

To smooth down all these rough edges, there is only one way. You will have to learn from the advice of St. Paul and be submissive. That means, literally, as we say in Italian, *sotto messo*—"placed under" so as to be the support of your family. You must be its foundations. You will sustain everyone, your husband and your children, by adapting, accepting, suggesting, and sweetly engaging. It is he (or in this case she) who is below, who holds up the world, not the person who places himself above others.

Only you will be able to do this, because in your family you are the only adult woman, meaning the only one who is flexible, gentle, solid, strong, patient, and far-sighted.

But enough of alpha females and omega males. You will also have to learn how to let go of the reins and overcome the temptation to be a control freak. You can't direct every operation, and you will have to make the extreme act of humility and faith of letting your husband get on with it sometimes. Even when you are 90 percent sure you are right. Try it. Try not to say, "I don't think so." Bite your tongue and have the courage to stand back and watch what happens when the world is deprived of your opinion. Things may not proceed in just the way you would have chosen, but, amazingly, the world will keep right on spinning. And he will begin to ask you your opinion, now that you no longer try to impose it on him. Handing over control also means making him the finance minister, and from the moment you start trusting him, you should resist the temptation to check the bank accounts all the time. Try not to make it like a budget meeting in Congress. Instead, give him your vote of confidence.

When you have to criticize him, do it with respect and without humiliating him, if you are quite sure that the criticism is indispensable. If you can wait, the morning after is always a better time.

When he has spent the last twenty hours painting the whole living room that lovely pearl-grey color you felt it really needed, try not to point out to him the drips on the parquet flooring.

When he spends the whole morning working on your car because you are totally inept—so much so that if the windshield washer tank is empty, you think it might be better to sell the car rather than learn how to refill it—at least don't give him a hard time for being late.

You are called Monica, like the first great wife-saint, the mom of one of the great minds of human history, St. Augustine. (Excuse me, St. Monica, could you please tell me as one mother to another what educational games you bought for your son?) She was a wife who waited with patience for years for her husband and son to come around, to understand.

With a patron like that, you won't disappoint us.

A kiss from your emergency friend,
C

Sometimes, when I ask my husband Guido for a particularly demanding proof of his love for me (you know the sort of thing: a train tour of churches I wanted to visit, hosting the kids' friends at our house, or putting up shelves) and I get, let's be clear about it, a definitive no, I remind him that he promised me eternal fidelity before God. I definitely heard it. I remember it well.

He replies that, yes, he probably was at my wedding—"my" wedding, of course—but he doesn't remember hearing or saying anything about "'til death do us part."

The cashier in the shop the other day said to us, "Are you together?" He replied, "For the moment, it appears so." He has made his own Harry's line from the film *When Harry Met Sally* about how he never went with his girlfriends to the airport, not even after their first red-hot date, so as to avoid them getting used to a high-maintenance lifestyle. Guido is a bit like that, not wanting to compromise himself . . .

To my question "Do you at least really like me?" comes the answer "Sometimes." On the other hand, I would tend to consider the fact that he has had four children with me in seven years a fairly significant measure of his—what shall we call it without exaggerating?—esteem and affection.

Contrary to the image presented in some places of marriage as the tomb of love—or "Go to bed with your wife in the absence of any alternative" and similar supposedly humorous clichés—to marry someone means entering into an ever new, dynamic, and demanding relationship. People say that as the years go on, there's a risk of habit setting in. I don't know about that. I can't wait to get bored!

But if it were to happen, I have a list, three pages long, of things to do. (I'll take it to my grave, I'm sure. Who will sort out, after me, the big box of kids' pictures? Who will read all those books? Who will brush up on Greek verbs? Who will run all those marathons I wanted to run? Who will call up all those people I still want to see, or at least hear?)

For as long as we live, it's difficult to imagine getting bored with life.

Marriage makes sense. It makes a huge amount of sense if it's a Christian marriage, because for those who ask for it, there's help from above, just like in those video games when you strike the enemy base and you get triple points—or so my kids tell me.

The help from above puts your heart aright and does away with the risk of life seeming sterile. That help from above allows you to see beyond the horizons of tiredness and difficulty, not through a sense of duty, but through a belief that you have banked all you had on the right choice.

And since struggle, suffering, and falling and skinning your knees are all ingredients on the menu of existence, you may as well choose the part of struggle. It's also helpful to choose someone to share a little bit of that struggle with, preferably not throwing yourself on them like dead weight. (Monica, when you are in a really bad mood, go out for a run, call someone—preferably not me—or take your frustrations out on the peanut butter jar if you must, but not on Domenico!)

Thus the path can be pleasant even amid the struggles of daily living, though I can't speak for my husband. Sometimes I let myself down, and I think, "He is happy, too." At that point in my mind, I see the image of myself, the sweet wife preparing his dinner with loving care and attention surrounded by the little ones. And then I have the terrible thought that he may actually prefer to be gyrating with a row of Brazilian dancers in skimpy outfits, blowing a party horn to the tune of "Brigitte Bardò Bardò"!

Breaking out of a revenge-type mentality certainly helps to foster a positive atmosphere, as one of my friends knows only too well—he is married to a woman who is so shortsighted that she objects to his love of mountaineering (a sport that has the distinct advantage of not being able to be practiced in the backyard and requiring a certain degree of travel away from the urban sprawl, and thus away from the nagging wife herself).

Or you find a lot of couples whose dominant model is that of the contract. "I looked after the kids to let you go and play soccer; you should look after them now and let me go to the gym." They seem more like a business partnership than a loving couple, and the danger is that businesses open and close depending on market conditions. That's part of the reason for the growing number of divorces, often where women have interfered with the old balancing acts—sometimes rightly so— but without having put proper alternatives in place.

In the old days, people got married for financial reasons and for security, and even if they didn't love each other, they probably respected each other. Now in the era of the dictatorship of emotions and feelings, the expectations of marriage are sky-high. Nowadays, for the union to endure, it must be happy, happy, happy. No longer do people "make do." I don't know whether it's right or wrong, but I do know that it's hard to satisfy so many expectations and changes. Especially if the partners are not prepared to put up with each other, to know how to wait, to seek out creative solutions—since they have said to each other, "In sickness and in health, in poverty and in wealth, 'til death do us part." And remember, we promise not only "to love" but also "to honor."

Women, in redefining their role, have called into question that innate talent that Cesare Pavese, the great Italian writer, defined as follows: "That original disposition, an absolute virtuosity in giving sense to the finite. The woman finds a way for herself and for man to be at peace with the world, she seems to be in harmony with existence in a way that man cannot understand, since the woman explains perfection, she is the deepest life of man: a tranquil and hidden life as the life of the roots always is."

What do you have to do to "be the life" of someone?

First I think it means bearing their burdens and weaknesses, being with them without feeling superior to them. There's a risk in that mentality of "I'll do it; I'm good at it," for it implies also the unspoken follow up: "And you're not." For example, I sometimes find myself passing harsh judgments about another person, judgments as piercing as any Jedi lightsaber, and if I'm being honest, when I am in crusading mode, it's best to avoid me. (My husband understands how to do this very well. At such times, he vanishes from sight, and his cell phone, even if he remembers to switch it on, seems mysteriously to be permanently in a no-service area.)

But even that's better than when we women play the victim card, presenting ourselves as resigned martyrs whose stigmata one expects to see bleeding at any moment. That's another of my specialties: I do it very well. I remain silent; I am moved by my own nobility of soul, by the magnanimous way in which I put up with everything—basically, by my own heroism. Recognizing the other person's limits—he or she has them, too—has to be done in a constructive way and not with a slow-witted passivity.

To "be the life" of another person means being attentive, showing little acts of tenderness and delicacy, remembering that the other person comes first. We tend to forget all of these things bit by bit as the years pass, cleaning babies' bottoms and correcting homework to the point of exhaustion, so much so that we don't even acknowledge each other as we walk by in the hallway.

One night I was so tired, I took my daughter into bed upside down, with her feet at my face and her head down under the covers, and I couldn't work out why she wasn't calming down even when she was being held. I was giving her energetic pats to help burp, but alas, the pats were on her legs rather than her back! I probably hadn't slept for a couple of nights and was so tired I didn't even remember my husband's name. (There was a man in my bed, that much I remember, but not very clearly because I was almost dead with tiredness.) Sometimes stopping to dedicate a bit of attention to that forgotten man at your side can be very dangerous. If you get out of practice, things get out of control—one of your children might end up going to school in their pajamas while another will be a second away from disaster as he tries to push a screwdriver into the electric socket. Despite all that, you need to find time to remember your spouse.

"To be the life" of the other person means taking care of the nest—that is, the house and the food. I think I can say I do that, if we overlook certain little habits. For example, I always remember too late that I have to make dinner. (Have you ever tried to defrost meat by breathing on it? Or by shoving it under your armpits?) And every so often, late in the evening, when I'm semiconscious through exhaustion, I try to put some order into the chaos of the house from a sitting position, trying to restore everything in its proper place through maximum concentration. It doesn't work.

"To be the life" of the other person means to love without measure, which means without counting the cost but doing so properly, loving him as he wants to be loved. So, for example, if he is tired and just wants a bit of time to himself, it is not a loving gesture to arrange for friends to visit—even if that's exactly what you would like.

It means being sensitive—not invasive but delicate. It means continuing to knock on the door, continuing to say thank you, continuing to respect the other person. Love can be a violent emotion, but the loved one is not your property.

"To be the life" of someone means a continuous effort at living and telling the truth, even if doing so doesn't require us to say absolutely everything to each other; there are some problems that would simply place a useless load on the other person's shoulders. But it also means not being afraid to expose ourselves to the other person. (Guido, can I take this opportunity to reveal something in front of everyone? Confession time: I have never understood the offside rule in soccer.)

It means accompanying each other as we journey towards the ultimate mystery, because in the end, our most intimate and profound essence is not to be found in being male or female but rather in that stamp of eternity, that desire for happiness, that thirst for the absolute that is in each of us.

Three Years Later . . .

You might be forgiven for thinking that Monica, after getting married, would stop assailing my ears with her doubts. (Yes, of course she got married. Have you not yet understood that a woman on the phone just needs to complain a little or receive a compliment—even a made-up encouraging one or an excessive one—anything rather than be taken too seriously?)

But alas, no, Monica is an Olympic champion of uncertainty. She is an artist in the area of tormenting her friends and an expert in the art of the tiring phone call. For a year, or a year and a half, she continued to ask me regularly, "Do you think I've done the right thing?" thus confirming the theory that the wedding day is not the magic moment that resolves all problems but the beginning of a new chapter in life. Indeed, if truth be told, during that first year of married life, the doubts became worse. I should get a special financial compensation in old age for being a friend of Monica's (if I ever make it to pension age), because our Dear Miss Perfect found an array of things about her husband to complain about. I think she has filed all her complaints in ring binders, everything from A (Always screwing on the lid of the coffee maker too tightly) to Z (Zealously swatting the mosquitoes all over the hall). And along the way covering everything from B (Bathroom flooded after shower) to M (My dear, you never listen to me when I'm speaking!).

But at a certain point, everything changed, I don't know exactly how, and if truth be told, I'm actually a bit jealous, because after years of listening to my advice, she seemed to get it—all on her own. She made a stunning U-turn. Monica decided to stop noticing only what Domenico did for her and tried to find a way to do something for him, forgetting herself a little. She decided to trust him and his way of doing things. She decided to look upon her husband with that look of hope that allows the other person to be himself in true freedom. Domenico now dotes on her, and if he loved her before, now he adores her—he is absolutely crazy about her. And this is a problem because for the last eight months, he's had to fight for her attention with another man. The other man has only two teeth, weighs eighteen pounds, and dribbles when he eats a cookie, but he is a formidable rival in love.

Chapter 2

Olivia and Lavinia

Or

My Girly Girls

Dear Olivia and Lavinia,

Let's pass over for now the fact that you're both my daughters, and let's also overlook the tiny detail that you are both still in preschool. I won't make any recommendations to you like I normally do throughout the day. Let's assume that I have already told you the following today: "Olivia, leave that pacifier alone," because now you are a "big boy," as you like to say— that is, big like your big brothers, one of whom is actually in fifth grade. And no, the horse in the garden doesn't seem to me like a very good idea. Yes, I know that a real princess is always saved by a charming prince, but if you were to concentrate on getting down from the bed without knocking your head, that would be a big step forward.

"Lavinia, don't kick things as you walk past in that careless way, and always remember that Mom always sees you—even when you're in the room next door." (Just as she will see you when you're older and traveling abroad and throwing away a cigarette in the street, for that matter.) And yes, I understand the fascination of that gold fountain pen that your grandfather gave me and that you always need for your homework and drawings, but if you were to use a more modest pen, I'd be very grateful.

And yes, I understand that when you're a girly girl, you really are a girly girl, but I do think we could allow a little leeway in terms of your outfits. Even if you're not wearing pink on the day you meet your handsome prince, it will not be a disaster!

Let's also take for granted that we, your parents, love you and your brothers even more than life itself. Your dad's heart melts when he looks at you—especially you girls! He has already prudently bought corny T-shirts that say on them, "One Day My Handsome Prince Will Arrive and My Dad Will Tell Him to Get Lost!"

It's true that you have made him do things that would have been unthinkable in the past. Things like getting you into a pair of tights in less than 15 minutes, or working out the difference between an eye shadow (that elegant shade of pink—very 1980s) and a lipstick, or learning how to rock on a hammock (for the truth is that wherever he is, you girls find him and spread yourselves over him).

Let's leave aside all the wonderful things that we could say about you—Lavinia's sense of humor, Livia's sensitivity, the intelligence of both of you, and all the other great qualities you have that we talk about in private. This is not the moment to go into them all.

Let's leave aside, too, all that advice that will become the soundtrack of your schooldays. Things like "You have to write out this page again from the top." Or "Did you pack your school bag?" Or "You know dad and I don't approve of those Winx cartoon characters or those dolls that say, 'I'm crazy about shopping!'" We're never going to buy them for you!

Let's also pass over the whole adolescence thing because I know that when the time comes, you will hate me and that everything I say will be taken down and used as evidence against me. (If you do have to use makeup, though, at least make sure that the eyeliner is the same color as the mascara.) And while I'm at it, when it comes to makeup, when you're grown up, remember the two basic principles: First, never go out without foundation. (Can we have a minute's silence for the fantastic guy who invented it and who deserves a Nobel Prize?) And second never give a Chanel makeup set to someone you have just stopped breastfeeding.

Let's pretend for now that you are both young ladies. I'm thinking through my second-worst nightmare—the idea of me dying before you guys grow up. My number one nightmare would be something happening to you. That would make my life utterly unbearable, were it not for the fact that we must always remember that life is not our own property, but is always safely held in the hands of that Someone who loves us so very much.

I don't know what the spirit of the age will be like when you begin to question yourselves about your identity. I don't know how much times will have changed compared to our day. Right now, it seems a lot for me to get my head around.

OK, maybe we *should* start with adolescence. If truth be told, most preadolescents make me feel like some kind of idiot, with their outfits, makeup, and attitudes that hint at a mysterious reality—namely, sex, which, at their age, I didn't even know the meaning of.

You are not to use expressions like (listen to who's talking) "I'm nervous—time to shop" at an age in which I went around with braces, orthopedic shoes, and clothes inherited from my cousin who was fatter and shorter than I was (I was a beanpole). If truth be told, I was a total mess, but I was too young to realize it.

Nowadays, even cartoons—which should be an escape and a protection from life's traumas, fears, and pain—are full of cheap allusions to sex, allusions that bombard you right from the cradle. Yes, even cartoons are full of love stories, romantic engagements, and handsome princes raining down from on high. And not watching television is not in itself a protection, because somehow you are reached by these messages in other ways.

Adolescence begins early and continues late, right into old age, in fact. I wonder when one should define oneself as being old? Should it be seventy (which is the new sixty)? Or maybe sixty (which is the new fifty)?

It's a question that has been doing the rounds since Gloria Steinem invented the original line. Nowadays you see forty-year-olds with Hello Kitty Smart cars, T-shirts decorated with gnomes, and necklaces of pink puppets. (OK, I have one too, but someone bought it for me and you guys quickly claimed it!)

Economic analysis is not my forte, even though I had ambitions when I was a writer, as Luca, my ex-boss, knows only too well. He always had to cut back on my digressions when I was writing a story for the television news—what profound and masterly pieces on the trends on economic consumption they were.

Select. *Delete.* That was the basic rule . . . "But Luca," I would cry, "you've cut out the best bit! You're clipping my wings!"

Every morning, he would reply without altering the inscrutable expression on his face (though I always thought he was smiling beneath that moustache), "If I don't clip your wings, you will end up like Icarus. You are supposed to be giving me the figures from ISTAT—the National Statistics Agency. I don't need a homily with them!"

So analysis is not my strong point, but now Luca no longer reads my output, and so I can give free reign to the economist in me that is fighting to get out. And so I wonder if all of this prolonged adolescence is not encouraged in some way—through publicity and the communication sector—by the laws of the market? It creates and increases dramatically an appetite for false needs and useless products, making things absolutely essential that a fifty-year-old should have long since forgotten.

But back to adolescence: If your father allows you out on your own before the age of thirty, the game of seduction will be at its strongest. It's the age at which you always feel you have to be "available" to capture *him*, the only boy in your field of vision who is not looking at you. It's a game of conquest that has very little to do with love and that forces you to make yourself noticed: good makeup, well accessorized, and always with something new (the rule goes something like this: "I like him because he does not want me"—typical functioning of the human brain at its most basic level).

Thus are produced compulsive consumers full of induced needs: The single woman with disposable income is the delight of every marketing director. Also popular are the DINKS—double income no kids—who also have loads of money to spend.

It's not that I am exalting poverty; riches are a blessing to be used with good judgment and proper criteria for our own good and the good of others.

So, girls, this is why you hear the word *no* so often (though not enough for your grandparents' liking) to your constant requests. It's about helping you understand as early as possible that our deepest needs are not satisfied with objects, even though sometimes I feel pretty certain that the Dior handbag in the shop window would bring me great psychological benefits! In fact in educating you, I educate myself, because, if truth be told, I am the sort of person who could find something meritorious in buying just about anything. Once I discovered a hat (have you ever seen me with a hat?) I think from the sixties in a tiny shop in a tiny village in the Marche region that carried an incredible assortment of items that would have been more at home in the kind of shop that closed a lifetime ago. I immediately asked myself how I could live without that hat and bought it. They must have toasted to my health after I left. And thus I ended up with a new, prestigious article to clutter up the house along with all the scarves, little notebooks, pens, purses, and other unused objects that at the moment of purchase seemed essential to my psychological and physical well-being.

After adolescence comes the study period. This is also extended these days: now you get a bachelor's degree, then the postgrad, the master's, the doctorate, the research grant, the internship, and so on. So it is that the entry into adult life, with its dramatic and brave decision to get a house of your own and start a family, are delayed ever more. And so if and when children arrive, they do so when the parents have the physical energy of mature adults (and the brain of adolescents).

As for sex, we'll talk at the right moment. I'll explain to you how not giving yourselves away is good, especially for you. You will never regret having waited, having taken your time, allowing the emotions to settle a bit. Sex can lead to new life—a new eternal life—and life is not something to be messed around with.

Breaking the link between making love and giving life has rendered sex empty and more cowardly instead of being adventurous and courageous. Giving love-making its true (enormous!) importance will make it vastly more precious and emotionally fulfilling for you.

In fact, surveys, newspaper articles, and opinion polls all show a generalized decline in sexual desire;

indeed, they talk about the death of sexual desire going hand-in-hand with an excess of satisfactions. You can understand this . . . think of what it's like when you use every trick in the book to get some gift or other, only to find that it quickly loses its attractiveness as soon as you get it. (Remember all those abandoned Barbie dolls? Remember the poor abandoned monkey toy lying forgotten at the bottom of the basket?)

Much later in life, we women begin to ask ourselves what we really want to be. The answer isn't nearly as clear as it was, for example, at the time of your great-grandmother, Irma, who in all her 96 years probably never once asked herself that question, because she was so caught up in supporting herself and her family.

To have the opportunity to ask ourselves what we want to be and to have a massive range of options laid out before us and not a one-way street to which we have been destined from birth is, without doubt, a great privilege for our generation, as is our freedom. But just as we need to learn how to make good use of wealth, so too do we need to learn to make good use of this freedom. In other words, there comes a time when you have to respond, make your choice, rebel against that childishness and the rhetoric of *sliding doors*—that other life we could have had if we had only got into a different car on the subway—which has made the fortune of a generation of modern writers.

In other words, girls, at a certain point, you'll have to make your choices and take responsibility for them. Not now, when you are still small, for now we can choose for you without discussion. (Just think, in about twenty years' time, you'll be able to make that decision to live without spinach!) I'm sorry to say it, but ours is not a democratic house. But being well trained and obedient will stand you in good stead when the time comes to make decisions of your own. You'll have understood, I hope, some clear sense of a concept that might now appear obsolete—right and wrong, good and bad.

I remember once a colleague said to me, with sincere sorrow and not a little indignation in his voice, "Do you mean to tell me that you think that what you believe is right and what I believe is wrong?" In his eyes, there was a genuine amazement. He was thinking, "But she is such a lovely girl." It wasn't as if I had said to him that I was going to hang around outside preschools handing out alcohol and pushing drugs! So yes, Renato, if you are reading this, I did mean it! No matter how incredible it may seem to you, I think that there is such a thing as right and wrong, not interchangeable concepts, no ifs and buts. Just think what a claim that was from his point of view . . .

But back to the question of identity . . . Those of us who were in high school in the 1980s thought we would grow up with everything we could want. We were sure we were men's equals. There was no difference between us and our brothers in the home or in the classroom. We studied without considering it any kind of victory to be able to do so; the idea of being able to become doctors, lawyers, and college professors was taken for granted, just as it was taken for granted that we could have everything, not only in our work lives, but in our personal lives too. We never thought that there would be a price to pay, that none of us would be able to be everything we might want to be and realize every dream.

So it was that when I was 15, my grandmother Gina—the great-grandmother that unfortunately you never knew—scolded me because I had served myself from the pasta bowl before serving my brother, Uncle Giovanni. I remember I laughed out loud. In the daily struggle for comfort in the house, which often involved elbowing my brothers out the way, mine wasn't a battle between the sexes but rather a battle for living space.

Grandma's idea was that at table, the women should sit down only after having fed the men, even when they themselves had been out working in the field all day. She had a soft spot for me—I almost always wear her earrings and her little statue of the Madonna always has a place in the house—but she considered me *marampta*, which in the dialect of our home city of Perugia means "lacking grace." I wasn't enough of the little housewife for her. Well, Grandma, you won't believe it, but I've now learned how to iron and take someone's temperature to within two-tenths of a degree just by feeling his or her forehead.

Nowadays, I would listen to what you had to say differently. Today, we women are no longer required to act as servants, but we can choose to serve each other out of love and as a freely chosen response to a call. Men and women are very different, which has nothing to do with equal opportunities. We are not the *same*, and not recognizing this is a cause of certain suffering, as indeed happens every time we deny the truth.

From Grandma Gina's time to my time and even more so your time, we've had the emancipation of women; the feminist battles, which were its driving force; and the almost obligatory insertion of women in the workplace. What we've forgotten is that you can't have everything in life: working outside the house like a man and staying at home like a woman.

Let's not regret all those changes, absolutely not. My grandmothers, when they were born, couldn't vote, and even as late as the 1960s, you would hear people say terrible things on television without fear of criticism, things like "Women are like meatballs; the more you batter them, the better they are." I know this because your dad always makes me watch RAI Storia, which is the Italian history channel. What a joy that is: no shows made after the 1970s. And just when you're in the mood for a romantic comedy, you get a documentary on the Roman suburbs of the postwar period! Never mind, such shows revealed to me that in the past, in order to choose what was considered a good wife, a man had to be certain that she "looked good, shut up, and stayed at home."

Let's not even talk about all of that. Thank God it's a million miles away from you and is not a threat to your life as adult women.

However, the reaction to those injustices has gone too far.

Feminism was in its own way flowering—an explosion of the need to feel loved, understood, and valued. It's just that it took the wrong path when it focused on the affirmation of self. At that point, we started to play the power game; in fact, we should have done away with that logic that we were protesting against. By "we," I mean our mothers and older sisters.

In the end, it ended it up worse for us. Emancipation—which started out as a claim for justice—led to a distorted idea of equality. Equality is not sameness. It is about giving equal dignity to two identities that could not be more different. You girls see it with your brother, don't you? In what ways are you alike, apart from the disorder, the love for hydrogenated fats and food colorings, and a certain talent in decorating with indelible stains any item of clothing or other textile with which you come in to contact, especially curtains, tablecloths, and cushions, especially the ones without removable covers?

Genesis—the beginning of the "Jesus book," as you call it—when it recounts the story of the creation of mankind in the image of God, says only this: "Male and female He created them." It doesn't say He created them as intelligent creatures, free beings with souls. None of those fundamental qualities is the first to be listed when describing our origins. Male and female. That's all.

There before anything else lies the root of our identity.

For a woman, her genius lies in welcoming. Feminism has denied this and, in doing so, has cheated us. Because when you betray your own nature, you go crazy, and I know many women like this (you know some of them too, but you're too little to realize it). They are sad, angry, disappointed, resentful, and jealous. They are divided in their inner selves.

They want to affirm themselves, but they deform themselves by going against their natural instinct to be welcoming. Our very physical makeup reminds us of this truth, the fact that we are able to make space for another person in our wombs.

Too many women are also at war with their husbands and become unbearable, and all because they haven't understood the secret of being welcoming and then of submission (in Italian, *sotto mettere* means to place under so as to be supportive), of obedience seen as an act of generosity.

"Bernardo, in your opinion, what do us females have in common with you males?" I asked your brother, whom, as you know, likes to enlighten us every so often with the philosophical wisdom of his eight years.

"We are all living beings," he replied after having reflected on it and conscientiously chewed on his chicken nuggets.

"But, Bernie, a tree is a living creature. We must have something else common!"

"I can't think of anything else," he replied, and with that cut short the discussion. Mind you, he is probably not best disposed toward the opposite sex due to excessive exposure to them and their noise at home and at school, surrounded, as he is, by mom, sisters, teachers, and little female playmates whom he finds annoyingly ebullient, he being a young boy of very few words.

So we are different from men, and I believe that when you ask yourselves who you want to be in life, you should bear this in mind. Your vocation to be welcoming will be realized and integrated into the life that you choose for yourselves rather than rejected or suffocated. At the moment, for the record, your standard responses to the question "What do you want to be when you grow up?" are "Ballerina" and "A doctor for horses." "But," as you say, Livia, "I also want to be the person who looks for head lice"—that is, a mom. Just as well, I'm supposed to be a model for you, and I hadn't realized that the art of eliminating parasites had struck you as my distinguishing feature.

So when all is said and done, what more can I say to you? My hope is that your generation of women can finally be at peace with itself, and I hope that you can fulfill your deepest identity by consciously choosing it. And so—and this really is an unfashionable wish—I hope that you will be, more than anything else, strong and thus welcoming, open to others and capable of bringing people together. In a word, if you can, be good.

With love,
Mom

There, I knew it, I've done it again. I have gone into televangelist mode. It happens every now and again, and it's not great for those who happen to be within range, especially if they are more than nine years old. But I can't do anything about it.

The fact is that I see all around me women who are suffering, or are certainly worried, searching for something, or unfulfilled—even when they appear to have everything.

Indeed, the more we have, the more we struggle (and here I have to use the plural) to keep everything together and to give up being a control freak and the tendency to be a perfectionist.

In my first years as a wife and mother, and by coincidence also my first years of work life, my cell phone, when switched on, said on the display, "You are late." I needed that reminder as soon as I woke up.

I think that before anything else, we need to take a step back in our personal life. Much is asked of us—too much. Emancipation has left us worn out and overburdened—work, husband, children, house, social life, and all the rest, which we know only too well. Quite simply, it's just not possible to do everything and to do everything while smiling, being in a good mood, and looking well groomed and elegant.

Dear me, let's not talk about grooming. To my hairdresser, for example, I'm like a pariah. I turn up twice a year with my hair in the most unbelievable mess, whatever is still straightened after a week of work, and then I always have to leave while my hair's still wet. There I am, silently taking advantage of that precious time (Sitting down? Not doing anything else? How often does that happen?), reading one of those sixty (or is it eighty?) books piled up on the shelf that give me dirty looks every time I pass by—though that's nothing compared to the disapproval of the hairdresser for my unruly hair.

At a certain point, you have to take a step back and accept with serenity that you might be late—more precisely that you might not be perfect.

I cannot think of any woman I know who doesn't complain about not having enough time to do all the things she has to do and so feels guilty about it. In fact, it can be useful to learn to do things in a much more relaxed manner, though if anyone knows how to do this, please tell me, because I have a habit of seeing every issue as decisive and nonnegotiable, every day as a European Cup Final, and every disagreement as disastrous.

Yet I learn each time that, to my great surprise, you almost always survive.

For example, I learned to my absolute surprise that none of my children have yet died because of a handful of bugs. You know the scene: While you are finishing cleaning the floor with a cloth, they come crawling over to you with a muddy shoe in their mouth (let's hope its mud). Or you realize that they somehow survive even if occasionally they eat absolute junk bought outside. Or you switch on the television to watch something that they really want to see and then collapse on the sofa because you are so tired. They survive, amazingly, even if for a whole year you are not on the school board and you miss a meeting about the new school curriculum—though I have to say, when I do go to these meetings, I secretly read something else under the desk because I always feel I need an interpreter to translate the school jargon. It's clear that we have to learn how to lower our expectations and, for those of us who are married, to trust the person we have at our side and his or her way of doing things (though I have to confess that my way of burning the soufflé is not shared by anyone else in our home). We have to learn to delegate, to give up being control freaks, and to choose to do without sometimes.

It doesn't work for women to search for security outside themselves—whether that be success in what they do, in men, through work, or through beauty—rather than searching for security in the God who is the only One truly able to offer it.

A woman gets lost when she forgets who she is. A woman is first and foremost a wife and mother. One who offers space and protection, and not only in the narrow confines of the family, for we women should be able to be companions and mothers to everyone who crosses our paths. In fact, if any of my wise and welcoming female friends wishes to adopt me, here I am! I am not proud; I wouldn't be offended by a remote adoption that might only involve delivering ready meals to the house. There are six of us, but I promise to give you back your plates properly washed!

As Edith Stein says, the soul of the woman should always be broad—that is, open to all; warm and luminous to help even the smallest plants to grow; full of peace because if it is stormy, little plants sometimes don't make it; reserved because sometimes external intrusions can be as dangerous as a whirlwind; and empty of self so as to create space because you need fertile land to grow something. She needs to be in charge of herself because she should be ready to be of service and not a slave of her own moods, which can be like a dark cloud on the horizon.

Our soul is certainly broad, as is evidenced by the interest we show in the lives of those around us—not always with the most noblest of intentions. Just think of that time when that friend of yours was about to hang up and you said, "Wait 'til I tell you this, but it stays between us"; you can be sure that your friend won't be hanging up any time soon. Not that you are talking ill of anyone, you understand; it's for her own benefit.

This is not exactly the kind of greatness of soul that Edith wrote so much about—she who before becoming patron saint of Europe with the name Theresa Benedicta of the Cross was an extremely able philosopher and pupil of Husserl.

A silent and reserved soul is not in our basic makeup, at least not in mine. My husband would testify to that since he never finds me quite as irresistible as when I have a 103-degree fever and I finally agree to succumb in silence and go to bed with an ice pack on my head.

We have to learn the art of silence; otherwise, we don't hear the weakest voices. Only by doing this, and really working at it, can we empty our souls of selfishness and avarice to leave room for others and to allow them to be heard.

We are certainly warm—too warm at times; sometimes our warmth is not very balanced. I am certainly like that. In a sense, men are more lucid, and we could learn from them.

But if we are not the ones doing the welcoming, no one will do it for us and no one else will take care of those entrusted to us. As Billy Joel says—a rather less profound sage than Edith Stein, but certainly easier on the ear—the woman can always bring out the best and the worst in a man (which of us hasn't felt that surge of pride at least once when listening to "She's Always a Woman"). The world is in our hands, and it is in a mess because we are lost. It seems very evident to me that in the area of human relationships, personal growth, and education, we are the ones who need to be keeping things on track and doing most of the work.

That's why if we go against our nature, relationships end.

Women who have experienced the ultimate betrayal—often victims of circumstances—and end up having an abortion find themselves bearing a great burden. These women are hurt and need tenderness because it is so painful to admit having made mistakes in life.

Together with them, all of us need to learn the gift of welcoming that transforms others—especially the man at our side. The woman at peace with herself knows how to love first. She knows how to listen, console, encourage, forgive, reunite, and create room for others. She brings tenderness to her family in her voluntary submission (back to that idea of being supportive). She builds up the father because she puts him above herself and gives him authority. She trusts because she knows him well and she is not afraid of losing herself and allowing the other person to win.

Three Years Later . . .

I would say that there is no subject in the world about which a woman is less calm and objective than that of her own children. I, for example, veer between peaks of motiveless pride (I knew he was a genius. I could tell from the way he looked at his little bees mobile from his cradle) and the depths of maternal anxiety (I have got everything wrong, I knew it. I shouldn't have refused to buy them that bag of Yu-Gi-Oh figures! Now they will suffer their whole life long).

Now that the older two are dangerously close to adolescence, I would quite like to enroll in a group along the lines of Alcoholics Anonymous at which I could stand up and say, "Hello everyone, my name is Costanza, and I am the mother of an adolescent" in the hope that someone not directly involved like myself might say to me (for a small fee, though I would be prepared to pay well) that we are doing a perfectly good job bringing up our children.

As for the recipients of this letter, who haven't yet read it ("It's too difficult, Mom!"), I can't say what kind of little ladies they will grow up to be. They should be OK in terms of self-esteem through lots of kisses, kisses, and more kisses and compliments, even though in every woman there is an almost unquenchable thirst for reassurance (even from God himself, who created that need and is uniquely able to fill it). If feminine genius lies in relationships and in looking after the other person, I would say that we are OK on that front too, judging by the girls' tendency to invite home just about anyone they meet; to set up emergency cradles for newborn stuffed toys; and to organize tea parties with tiny cups for friends, dinosaurs, and Barbie dolls in the course of which they dispense their advice at random.

It certainly seems to me that despite the passage of only a few years, the context in which they are growing has changed. There has certainly been an explosion in the means of communication. There is a campaign of ideological carpet bombing taking place in the media, pushing new gender theories and spreading the idea that no one has a given, sexual identity; that nothing is natural or unnatural; and that everything is a free choice. No longer are there male and female characteristics but only "orientations," so they are growing up in a period of anthropological warfare between two distinct visions of the world. I am sure that my little girls Livia and Livinia will fight for the right to say that being male and female is a good thing. I can see them in the battlefield now, clear-sighted, strong, and wearing beautiful breastplates . . . which will probably be pink.

Chapter 3

Marco

Or

Break on through to the Other Side

Dear Marco,

You are the living proof that the theory in *When Harry Met Sally*—namely, that men and women can't be good friends because sooner or later sex will get in the way—is mistaken. True, it happens quite rarely. But you really are one of those friends of the warm and comforting variety that you simply can't do without. You were the kind of childhood friend to whom people confided their deep romantic angst. (I do confess, however, to being officially offended that you never once showed any romantic interest in me!)

You, in exchange for sincere affection and trust, offered us that precious commodity—a male point of view, the echo of another planet, traces of life from a faraway galaxy.

We could ask you anything, a male viewpoint on our issues with our thighs, our hair, the length of our skirt, issues that your fellow males are totally disinterested in—that is, unless they have a direct and personal interest in the areas in question!

Indeed, with heroic self-denial, you were even ready to listen to how I felt about the tone of voice someone else had used to answer me. You were a martyr to friendship during all those hours you listened to me during some crisis of jealousy or other. You exposed and agonized over nonproblems with me, when your fellow males would have struggled to even manage a consoling pat on the shoulder. You even prefer talking to me, or another one of your lengthy list of female friends, rather than emit the inarticulate grunt that is the usual sound coming from the mouths of your fellow men as they watch whatever match is on television involving a spherical object being moved about in whatever direction through space.

I'll use this argument in my summing up of your cause for canonization—you hardly ever take offense.

For this reason, and because I do love you as a genuine friend (I've told you that for ages, haven't I?) I have to ask, why don't you and Chiara get married?

Probably because you have been living together since time immemorial, and not being believers, there's no particular reason for you to ask the blessing of a God whom you don't think exists on your union, nor do you feel the need to make your situation "official" in the eyes of the state.

Well, leaving aside all the polemics and bad feelings aroused by recent political campaigns about civil partnerships, you must know only too well that nonmarried people are at a great advantage in many ways. For example, for reasons that seem to me utterly impenetrable to a normal brain, unmarried parents have a much better chance (because they don't add together their joint income) of getting state family allowance for their children—note the bizarre choice of name for the benefit—than a married couple.

The time has come for you to marry Chiara and stop trying to leave every door of possibility open for yourself. You have to stop looking around with that vague look, planning some mad scheme to open a creperie in Paris or a sushi bar in Manhattan. What a great idea that would be! Why not a hot dog stand in Munich while you're at it?

All of this is just fantasy, Marco. It's not real life; it's the halo of emotion that surrounds real life. Have you ever done anything serious about any of these ideas? Have you asked for any kind of permits? Have you drawn up plans? You keep saying that you don't want to die as an employee of your firm, but you don't lift a finger to do anything other than open your paycheck at the end of the month.

I think you may have seen too many movies. You seem to be somehow convinced that heading off to foreign climates and doing something you have never done before would open up new horizons for you to conquer. Personally, I believe there is no more pioneering horizon to conquer than bringing a new life into the world and bringing up a child as God wills.

And forgive me for saying this to an old rocker like yourself, but your beloved Doors have had their day!

"Break on through (to the Other Side)" might have had some relevance in America in the 1960s, but not now. Now, I have to remind you of this, the real *other side* is committing yourself to caring for another person forever—your children, for example. The really risky option is to spend your life doing serious things, not idly indulging your desires. Explain to me what's so heroic and danger-fraught in doing exactly what you want to do? Everyone's pretty good at that. Serious involvement, not escapism, is the real act of transgression.

It's all very well to shout about breaking on through to the other side when you are Jim Morrison on Venice Beach in 1967. It's something quite different—though few people have a sense of this ridiculousness—to be doing so when you are Mr. John Smith, resident of Nowheresville, not to mention when you are Marco, trying to walk on the wild side of the little seaside town of Ostia Lido!

If you have to throw everything away, at least do it properly. Do it with some style, with class. Sell all that you have and head off without looking back. Risk something!

With you, though, while you toy with the idea of taking off—a very male way of thinking—you feel sorry for yourself and don't appreciate all you have. You have an intelligent woman at your side (and please stop sniffing around other women, because you know that if Chiara gives up on you, you're dead!). You've got an interesting job, even if you are always going on about the boring routine that makes you sick. I don't disagree, you are good at what you do and could do much more than is usually asked of you, but tell me which job doesn't involve some less-than-creative and enjoyable elements? And give thanks that you are not, I don't know, a guy who has to stack shelves in the supermarket or a new graduate working away in a call center. Even the great artists probably had to do some boring jobs at times. You can't always be writing Beethoven's Ninth Symphony.

I do admit that for you and Chiara, it may actually be quite difficult to be married, even though you have been living together for years (or maybe because of that). Because it does change things. It means locking the front door, and even if you can always escape, it is all about a new way of thinking, a definitive and irrevocable way of thinking. I have only one life, and I entrust it into the hands of this person. I surrender. It is a scary idea if you think about it.

I understand you. I was the last person of our age group to get a proper job, and I am the only one of the people who had been working on a short-term contract who didn't celebrate being taken on full time—not even a cake in the newsroom. A full-time permanent contract—how alarming!

But in your personal life, it's quite different. Nothing can substitute for the fruitfulness of a definitive choice. I could list endless differences between you and Chiara. Because differences there are, however much you two, the classic postfeminist couple, proclaimers of nondifference, might try to deny it.

I, who have two boys and two girls, can assure you that from the first cry from a baby's mouth, differences emerge.

I remember well when my little daughter Livia, the most obedient child who ever existed, became quite unstoppably hysterical after a dramatic encounter with the object of her desires. We were at the shrine at Loreto, where I had gone to pay a debt to Our Lady. She was a year old, couldn't speak, and could barely walk. From her stroller, she began to cry out, trying to get close to the shop window of her dreams: It was a window full of rag dolls.

After a year of third- or fourth-hand toys, dragons and hairy monsters, rubber blocks and construction sets, which I had imagined would work as well for her as they had done for her older brothers, here she was finally choosing something just for her. She saw a doll to hug, to take care of, to feed. Obviously, it was impossible to resist her pleas, and so Livia got the first in a long series of little beings to be nurtured with cups of pebbles and leaves from the garden.

Tell that to the feminists who deny the existence of a maternal instinct.

Her sister, on the other hand, has a soft spot for poor unfortunate princesses in search of a husband, and she, constantly dressed as a bride, waits patiently for the numerous male visitors to our house, mostly bold young men between 7 and 11. After all, you never can tell! Her dress is a filthy and worn-out garment that I have to wash secretly, hoping that her knight in shining armor doesn't show up during the final rinse.

They're different in everything: The boys come to church huffing and puffing, the girls follow me quite happily, even though, like typical women, they give me a hard time if I'm not smart enough: "Mom, you can't go and see Jesus without any makeup on!"

Let it not be thought that I am some poor soul, an "unliberated" type who administers stereotypes through her milk. The truth is I set out the same way with each of them. I've spent whole afternoons trying in vain to introduce those fine sons of mine to the joys of reading. But before I knew it, the girls' room had become a galaxy of pink satin, decorations, and sequins, while the boys' room had become an arsenal.

And all of this while I, a nonexpert mother, was reading self-help books, whose only purpose seemed to be to convince me that it was my fault if my child wasn't playing Mozart or writing some masterpiece while sitting on the potty. All the while the children were developing the character that had been given to them by the Creator.

You want to read them the Bible and Tolstoy's short stories. The older ones, I have to say, are both good readers, and I can't complain, but I've had to accept that no printed page can compare with the PlayStation, which is truly a joy to be savored for the kids. But even that joy is nothing compared to the BB gun. And the most irresistible of all are Granddad's real rifles. Not long ago, after his first day out hunting, Tommaso came home happier than I had ever seen him.

And the differences that manifest themselves in early childhood do not, in my experience, fade as the children get older. An adult male has the eye of a hunter, which may come in very handy if he happens to come across a woodcock in the corridor, but it seems to prevent him ever being able to find the butter in the fridge. And let's not even talk about how the shopping list with the words "Remember to buy yogurt" left very visibly on the center of the table seems invisible to his "hunter's eye." (I suspect because for some people in my house, yogurt is not considered a family essential!)

On the other hand, a woman's eye, which is somehow blind when it comes to map reading, can spot at a thousand paces from the stage the wedding ring on the guitarist's finger, mostly because the issue of whether a man is spoken for or not seems to us to be a vital piece of information.

When things go badly, you like to close yourself in your lair and be left in peace, so that if Chiara asks if you want to talk things over, you break out in a rash! She, on the other hand, wants to share with you all her worries. She wants to dissect and analyze and unburden herself of the weight of all those problems that, if truth be told, she will forget when the conversation is over, while you keep ruminating over them, trying to find a solution for her. After all, "Me Tarzan. You Jane" also means you feeling obliged to try to come up with a solution to her problems and providing for her, bringing home the captured prey, and protecting the nest.

Chiara always wants to check things and make plans; you would rather that things just happened. Though in my humble opinion, certain things don't just happen—things like paying the cleaning service or the kids' soccer fees. Obviously, I'm on Chiara's side on this one; she's like me. Some things simply can't be left to chance; they need to be regulated efficiently.

I admit you are abnormally impractical. Every time I think back to the efforts the 13-year-old version of you made to pack his backpack properly, I ask myself why the teacher was so cruel and didn't help you, why none of us helped you put your snack in your lunchbox.

The great adventure of getting new glasses was, for you, I seem to remember, a Herculean effort and allowed you to display manly courage and self-denial and a brave dismissal of the dangers of the enterprise—not only did you have to turn up on time for your appointment with the optician, you then had the follow-up visit to have the spectacles manufactured and fitted.

So Chiara bears all the burdens of running your household, and despite this—or maybe because your mind is empty of all such worries—you feel free to show off in front of that good-looking colleague of yours and offer her your shoulder to cry on for periodic sharing sessions, so much so that when asked about it, you rudely respond to Chiara, "We actually spoke about you too . . ."

Of course you males have to feel free, and Chiara, who is not a stupid woman, knows it and pretends not to know what's going on in your head.

It's this same low-cost approach to risk, this incapacity to leave behind current reality (which would be a sign of maturity) that causes you to dream, depending on whichever is the most recent documentary you have seen, of heading off to become a shepherd in new Zealand or a fisherman in Reykjavik.

Where are you going in life without any professionalism, other than that relating to your job? A job, I might add, which you would do well to learn to love and really treasure. Your problems are the nonproblems of a generation, actually of a privileged section of our generation who have never had to cope with questions of survival and subsistence. Of course it's great that we have all we need to live on, and I certainly don't want to hark back to the days when children were sent to tend the sheep at the age of six, leaving school behind. But at least appreciate how lucky you are! And appreciate Chiara too. What other woman would put up with all your moans and feel responsible for your moods and your serenity? When you men feel down, you really feel down, while for us women (and especially for moms), a bad mood is a luxury, one that we can't allow ourselves. For a mom, a carefree day, a day off, a pleasure break . . . these things are just not in the script!

The list of differences between you could go on forever, but what I want to say to you is this: You are both fully signed-up members of the "equality in a relationship" ideal. You are both reborn feminists. But this has led to you being immature. You don't like taking clear, definitive decisions. If you are equal, what are you doing with each other apart from satisfying certain nonessential needs? You are certainly not becoming unique and irreplaceable to each other.

You are not growing, you are not bringing together those spaces in each of your lives, those seeds of salvation that exist in equal measure but very different forms in man and woman, and you don't even seem to want children. There's a real serious link between these two issues.

I certainly won't be lending you a child to change your nappy when you grow old. You have to think now about these things. It will soon be too late!

Go ahead and get married, for goodness sake, and have children. If you don't it makes no sense to carry on together. You might as well go your separate ways and enjoy yourselves. A new woman every night for you. New idiosyncrasies, new panics, new ways of arguing. You can't be together for 15 years and not produce anything.

How do you actually measure a year in your life? By dawns and dusks? By cups of coffee—as sung by the Broadway bohemians of the 1980s? How do you know when a year has passed? A year should be measured by the number of times you've put aside your own preferences so as to give yourself to another person. It's measures in the life that you have transmitted to another person—not necessarily a son or daughter, but someone smaller than you, weaker, poorer.

It's not enough to be the bosom buddy of so many people—including people as marvelous and world-class as me! You deserve to be everything to somebody, because you really would be something very special. If truth be told, you have many talents, many gifts that I haven't focused on here. It's just that every now and again, I go into "old-fashioned mom" mode, which involves me seeing it as part of my sacred duty to list all the areas you could improve in. Think of what it's like for my poor children, who can't escape. You at least can see it as a sign of affection. If I say these things, it's because you are very special to me.

Your friend from the "other race,"
C

You see it often, a traumatized father trying to cope with a bossy four-year-old who is demanding categorically to be allowed to play on a ride that is way too dangerous for his age. The child self-combusting in fury while the dad—allegedly the head of the family—gets on his knees to do a deal with the child whereby he or she will get down from the dangerous ride in exchange for seven more rides on the pink elephant. At such times I ask myself, what has become of fathers?

I ask myself that question when I see adult males being abused by children—on some rare occasions actually being kicked and other times verbally abused—while the kid escapes scot-free without even disciplinary slap. I see little children willfully ignoring their parents instructions, leaving the mother and father shouting the child's name twenty times as they try to persuade the ungovernable little brat to get out of the swimming pool. And when, finally, the adorable little Matteo decides to obey, the parents never throw his latest video game into the nearest stream to remind him who is in charge. I reflect on all this on the beach when I see the amazement on the faces of the people under the neighboring umbrella at normal children who obey, not always willingly or smilingly, but nevertheless respond to what is asked of them.

I wonder who will ever speak to children about such things as courage or honor—certainly not that traumatized father. Who will read to them *Cuore* (a classic Italian children's novel written by Edmondo De Amicis) or *The Paul Street Boys* (a Hungarian children's adventure novel by Molnar Ferenc). Who is going to tell them about Nemecsek (a character in the latter novel) who dies rather than fail in his duty.

I can't tell how my own children will end up—probably more or less normal. I decided long ago to give up on the idea of having geniuses around the house or child prodigies, because the aim of this life is to get to heaven, not to win a Nobel Prize, not even to succeed. Maybe they will open a hardware store and it will be a great success (let's just hope they don't call it something sad like Not Only Screws or something pretentious like the Washer Boutique). The point is that if I, or even better, my husband, says to them, "Off you go," off they go without the discussion going on for hours.

"How do you do it?" I've been asked. I don't know why people always say, "I'll count to three," but never reach three, and I don't know what would happen if they did. In our family, it's quite simple. The children know that we have a few clear ideas; we don't consult them about every decision we make, and we have somehow gained some credibility. Occasionally, we may make use of some symbolic punishment, but more important we spend lots and lots of time with them.

You can't make them obedient from a lying down position under a beach umbrella; you can only make them listen to you by putting in a lot of dedication and goodwill, unless you achieve it with violence, and that's no way to operate.

One of the fundamental principles of life—you are what you do—can be verified quite easily with young people. Because they put into practice what they see actually happen, not what they hear preached to them. They hear with their eyes. For example, I can elucidate quite complex theories to them about the importance of eating properly at meal times, but if I do it through a mouthful of cheese I happen to be snacking on, it loses its meaning. It's the same if I graze while cooking and at the same time tell them not to eat before dinner. It's strange; when I think of it, I always seem to contradict myself when it comes to eating.

In the same way, it's no use issuing formal certificates of pride in a child's achievements if you spend every moment criticizing everything they do; and it's no use shouting at a child, "Don't shout!" Nor can you slap children into learning that they mustn't lift their hands in violence against other kids.

Authority comes from recognition of credibility in the one issuing the order. Not that I'm any good at it. I make an announcement at home such as "Everybody at the door in three minutes with shoes on and coats on." By the time the ultimatum has come and gone, there is someone flopped on the sofa nibbling, someone combing a Barbie doll's hair, someone listening to music, and someone determined to finish off a manual exploration of his nostrils. At such times, it occurs to me that I must run for president next time around—what an effective leader of men I am!

Luckily, with their father, things are different. If he speaks, they listen to him.

The truth is, it's up to fathers to reclaim their rightful role, willingly and with determination. And for once, the responsibility here lies not with the woman but with her companion.

The fathers of today have to roll up their sleeves and find a way to show authority.

Yes, a father can be a fantastic horse for a young Zorro to ride; he can fight with lightsabers; he can allow his hair to be combed by would-be hairdressers; and he can even kill spiders, chase ghosts, and prepare marvelously unhealthy snacks, but his first role, rather than moaning about not being able to breastfeed (as I have heard more than one man do), must be to guide the family, to point out the path, to provide a direction of travel, and to monitor it every day, setting limits and offering reassurance.

It's good to try to share objectives and agree on decisions, especially when the children are a bit more grown up, but on occasion, you also have to know how to insist. Because in response to the question "What do you think, Andrea, old pal, should we do our homework?" there is not a child on this planet who will reply, "Yes, of course." It's the same when you ask them, "What do you think, is it time to go home?" when they are shouting themselves hoarse with their friends during a game of tag. Or again, "Andrea, pal, what do you think, is it time to go to bed?" when Andrea is doing any activity at all, even cleaning the grout between the bathroom tiles—because for a child, anything is preferable to bed at bedtime.

Yet I hear ever more often parents ask their children's opinions about things that are the parents' responsibility to decide.

All of this comes from the basic idea spread by the Enlightenment, which is now dominant, of the basic and total goodness of man. If you think that the little being in front of you, in the right conditions, will be able to find within himself or herself the strength to always choose the right thing, what's the point of authority? In such a worldview, society would regulate itself.

To put this self-regulation to the test, we could offer to a party of six-year-olds a plate of chopped raw vegetables and one of sweets full of artificial colors and ask them to choose what's best for them. Or we could try suggesting, in front of a big box of toys, "Stand in a line and each of you take one toy, thinking of the person who comes after you." Or we could try saying, "Turn off your PlayStation. It's time to dedicate yourself to reading this very interesting section of Virgil's *Aeneid*."

Those who advance such theories have never seen children scratch each other's eyes out to get their hands on a toy car that is slightly bigger and shinier than their own and therefore must be grabbed. They have never seen sweet little blond girls tearing apart soft toys. They have never seen kids showered with gifts go off in a sulk because their brother received a cool present too.

Such people have never looked properly at adults with real intellectual honesty. They have not noticed as people try, at least for a day, to combat their bad inclinations, trying to be decent citizens, sometimes having to wear a mask to cover, to a greater or lesser degree, the cesspool within.

This is sometimes required because in other circumstances, the previously mentioned adult spends all his or her energies, from morning to night, trying to get the maximum gain in life with the minimum pain. That involves everything from cutting off cars when merging to doing work poorly or delegating it to a colleague (that gives you more time to gossip about the person who's not at work today).

And so it goes, with a long list of bad actions that don't require much imagination—evil is quite banal. But we behave this way with great tenacity and consistency to quench the thirst that we all have for power, for privilege, for comfort. When you think of it, if you boil all these things down, they essentially consist of a desire for approval and for love. The truth is that we all carry within us that little seed of evil that we Catholics call original sin. It's the only way to understand the mentality of the world. Our task as Catholics is to try throughout life to find a kind of creative disobedience to that tendency.

This struggle for freedom from evil and for true happiness gives sense to our lives. And we have to try to learn how to carry on this struggle to our dying day and try to teach it to our children from their very first day. And we do so not only because we hope for reward in the life to come but because this is how to live happily in the here and now. And we believers say that without God, a good father who is always on our side, we can't win.

Nowadays we are incapable of transmitting these truths because we don't possess them ourselves. Today, *doubt* is the watchword for many. To say that you have no certainties in life makes you seem somehow intelligent.

Honestly, I really like men with strong opinions and a powerful and brave demeanor. I don't know, maybe I'm not typical, because I see very few such men. Obviously, they are a product that's not much in demand these days!

But back to fathers and their role: They can't drive around with a sign on the back of their car reading, "Don't follow me, I'm lost too." That should be banned by law! And if dads have no certainties in their lives, they should quickly find some as soon as their son (or daughter) leaves the maternity suite.

The trouble is that modern man is lost, both as a man and also as a father.

It's probably the result of other changes—social, economic, political, psychological, whatever. Call in an expert to define it if you want. But however you define it, it seems to me that too many men are in the middle of an identity crisis.

"Do you know what the new summer look is for men this year?" my sister asks me. She is calling from a rather more fashion-obsessed vacation destination than mine, which is frequented by families from upstate Nowheresville. They arrive (actually, *we* arrive—I can't be too snobbish about it!) on the beach with six trunks full of sand pails and shovels and a cooler filled with food, enough to feed an entire bowling team!

The truth is I don't know what this year's summer look for men is. We didn't pose the question at the watermelon fest that is August on an Italian beach. For us, the big attraction of the year was the water gun, just as it has been for the last 15 years.

"It's the fins that are the big thing in men's beachwear this year," my sister reveals to me from the noisy resort from which she's talking.

"What?" Did she say rinse? The rinse is the big thing? Are we talking about rinsing men's swimming trunks? It doesn't strike me as a great fashion breakthrough; my husband certainly rinses

out his trunks (which go right down to his knees) after swimming, since the salt water irritates his skin. His trunks are the
same style my father-in-law wears (and has worn in all the years I
have known him). Could these be the big fashion breakthrough?

"No!" comes the exasperated reply. "I didn't say 'rinse.' I said
'fins'—you know, like fish have fins? It's a new cut in men's swim-
wear . . . a kind of push-up effect. They put a seam—or fin—in
the front part of the swimming trunks, which gives a particular
look to the 'contents,' shall we say. A more aerodynamic look,
apparently, which properly emphasizes the dimensions."

I'm sorry, maybe it's my age, but I find men like that about as
exciting as the hood of an old van. Shiny, rounded, but utterly life-
less. I don't know what percentage of men are affected by this new
approach to their bodies or whether it's mostly just the young.

The fact is that I am discouraged when I see so many young
men all done up, vain, with a slight hint of the feminine about
them; guys who clearly have regular sessions at the beauty
parlor—more regular than mine, for sure—to make sure their
waxing regime is in order, fitted in between hours and hours
spent at the gym. To me a man like that reminds me of a pranc-
ing peacock, or as they say in my home town of Perugia, they are
"as shiny as a show dog."

I suspect that there is a link between all this loss of identity,
all the various types of transgender stuff, metrosexual males and
effeminate-looking guys with their push-up swimming trunks
and the loss of a shared, solid sense of fatherhood. But I admit I
just don't know what the link is . . .

Three Years Later . . .

Marco has left Chiara and asked another woman to marry him.
I hadn't a clue about it before it happened.

What it proves, and I admit it, is that I am completely hopeless as a matchmaker.

As soon as a male under the age of ninety and a woman of childbearing age who is not already spoken for cross my radar, I try to match them within 15 minutes of the start of the conversation—at the point when they are still politely discussing the olive served with the aperitif. I interrupt them with a phone call to ask if they have a fixed wedding date. Obviously, my matchmaking efforts never work.

What is true is that I have never seen Marco as happy as he is now. The woman he is about to marry has come through a very difficult period, and he has decided to be at her side, shouldering with her the difficulties she faces. He has gone from being a little boy to a man. He has stopped messing around in life and has begun to take it seriously. He is now strong, solid, protective, decisive, and generous. I could never have foreseen this happening. A guy who could not put his books in a backpack on his own has taken control of not only his own life but that of a woman, with great courage, and has shown he is prepared to risk all.

What can I say? I had it all wrong, but I have never been happier to admit it. I think the change was that Marco met a woman who had the humility to say, "I need you," and this brought out in him the desire to behave like a man, to take on his responsibilities, to run risks, and to be responsible.

I wanted to call him to preach to him a little sermon about the beauty of the Cross, the fruitful grain of wheat, about losing one's life to find it . . . but for once, I said nothing, or rather, I said simply that I was very happy for them. I think Marco appreciated that.

CHAPTER 4

AGATA

OR

A TALENT FOR MR. WRONG

Dear Agata,

You are a "real woman," as a colleague of mine from Naples once described me by way of a compliment. Maybe he was more impressed by my report on the Icelandic economy than he was by my backless top, but hey, who cares? What I care about is you—and why a "real woman" like you doesn't have a line of men ready to do anything to have her as their own, to marry her, to whisk her off to their castle on their gallant steeds.

Why are you not engaged, or married, or indeed a mother, which is, after all, what you really want to be?

It's true that a woman's judgment about what men like is notoriously untrustworthy, as I have had occasion to note several times when I have spotted a certain smile hidden under my husband's moustache that he struggles to hide. He is trained not to give injudicious compliments! His training package also involves him providing a series of standard responses to my questions, which he can deliver even without turning his head to look at me. So for example, in response to the question as to how I look, he is trained to say, "Darling, you are really slim." (After all, a woman, as Coco Chanel put it, is never too rich or too thin.) Alternatively he will say, "You are beautiful even without makeup," if I ask him if I have time for a quick restoration job on my face.

Men's and women's views on beauty are just so different. "How vulgar!" I say to my colleagues in the newsroom as a certain amply proportioned beauty appears on screen. "Absolutely," they agree consolingly, "very vulgar."

"The Charlotte Gainsbourg look is much better. More flat-chested, a slightly irregular nose, but absolute elegance," I suggest.

"You're quite right, elegant in a flat-chested way," they grunt while not taking their eyes off the creature on screen, who has a vaguely piggy face and a chest that is frankly quite offensive to normal women like me.

So you see, I don't understand much about men's tastes, but if I were a man, I would ask you to be my wife ASAP, if anyone still uses such formal language!

You are beautiful, intelligent, good company, and friendly, and you have a healthy sense of irony. I simply cannot understand why you are not distributing those little numbered tickets—please take your turn—to men desperate to take you out to dinner.

Nor can I understand your unique ability to always pick Mr. Wrong. You seem to be able to spot such guys while they are still miles off in the distance. You head straight for them in a collision course, taking every precaution so that your impact is perfectly timed.

But despite all that, I do feel the need to share with you some lessons I've learned at the school of adult womanhood . . . like the art of applying your eye makeup in such a way that it gives you that perfect look. And then there's the other golden rule: "If the shoes hurt you in the shop, they'll always hurt you." And the classic, "It doesn't matter if you put on your nail polish, if you go out dressed like that, it's like putting a tie on a pig!"

You are the best style consultant any of your friends could ever have because you actually have a sense of style—unlike me, who, every six months or so, stops off at a shop on the way to work and picks up as many black or grey items that I can carry in 42 minutes with the notion of combining them with something brightly colored (which I don't own and never seem to buy).

You even pull off class hips that sometimes are a little on the large side, but that doesn't stop you elegantly wearing Parisian stockings and boots. You know what you're doing; you've always got just the right accessory and the right shoes—that's how you spot style, I'm told—to brighten up a pair of boring jeans and a turtleneck sweater. You are always able to engage in a pleasant and indeed brilliant conversation—it might not be the most profound, but you admit that yourself. You may not have got around to Benedict XVI's work on conscience, but you've read all the novels of the year. And when it comes to films, well, there's no competition.

You know how to succeed in society—you went to the right schools, you've traveled, you go out with human beings over eight years old, and you can propose a toast for someone's birthday in front of a crowd of thirty people who have nothing in common without a blink and without losing the attention of any of your audience. (Please never ask me to do that! I'd be happy to compose thirty hand-written letters to the guests—what fun!—but I am no good at toasts.)

If, when we are together, we meet someone "who matters," you always manage to give such a good impression of yourself, while I give the worst. Actually, to be accurate, I almost always end up saying nothing, which may not be so bad. Though if you only knew what sparkling conversation comes to mind when I am at home two or three days later . . .

You know just how to get out of any awkward personal or professional impasse. If it were up to me, I'd send you to do live television reports from wherever, for whatever event, because you'd always find something relevant to say, while I always panic a little when someone says they saw me on television for fear that they are about to tell me that I had spinach in my teeth when I was on air.

You know how to tell the truth without offending anyone (almost always); you know how to laugh at yourself and at others with the same lightness of spirit. You even know how to fall over stylishly, as I witnessed when we were in the mountains last year, while I would never attempt any sport that requires more coordination than is needed to put one foot in front of the other. Apart from running marathons, I think my only option is cross-country skiing. My preference is for slow, boring sports, and I don't get out of bed for anything shorter than 25 miles.

You, on the other hand, have the most laid-back approach I have ever seen, an almost Jamaican approach to life! "Take it easy," you like to say with a certain Anglo-Saxon pragmatism, not like me, who is always setting off, spear in hand, on some impossible mission.

You don't seem to give off that "looking for a husband" look that scares off the average man these days. Only those who know you well know that it is only now that you are beginning to open your mind to the possibility.

So it is that I ask myself how you have managed to have quite a run of disasters in love.

It is almost as though you were doing a doctorate on how *not* to succeed with the Italian man, or maybe someone offered you a lot of money to study the market in depth?

You have managed to find for yourself, without spending vast sums of money or leaving home, some of the worst examples of manhood on the market.

Just from memory, there was the lawyer with the Porsche who seemed like a character actor with his obligatory long hair, bronzed complexion, and odd clothes. He always dressed as though his main aim in life was to get his picture taken for the "Society" columns of the Roman newspaper *Il Messaggero*. Every time I met the two of you, I could almost see enormous neon-lit signs that read, "wimp" above your head. A bright future as a betrayed wife could have been yours, though as a consolation prize, you undoubtedly would have been able to cry your eyes out on a 13-seat Roche Bobois sofa in bright Roman red and make your chamomile tea in a rather splendid Bulthaup machine.

Then in a swift U-turn, you switched to the tormented intellectual type, one of those painful loves that left you in agony! Thankfully, you escaped before spending your whole life crying on filthy little sofas while he passed the day in love with some new high-tech gadget beginning with the letter *i*. Compared to that fate, I think I would rather my husband betrayed me with a blonde—at least then you could wait for her outside her house.

Then there was the guy who was separated from his wife, who was really very handsome but had three adolescent children who would quite happily have inserted pins into your eyes. He was brilliant and funny but just never around. Every second weekend away, the Christmas holidays booked, and the month of August and every Wednesday sacred to his family, and you would never have been able to be part of that. The shadow of the first wife always loomed large. You might have thought that he wanted to take things slowly with you, not rushing into anything, but the truth was that he had no intention of becoming involved in a new family when he had just disengaged himself from the last one.

Come to think of it, there was also that guy who was a "mamma's boy." I don't want to say too much against him, being a bit of a jealous and possessive mother myself and living in fear of what a terrible mother-in-law I will be. All I can hope for is that my friend Agata will be on duty to put me in my place. That place will involve knitting little sweaters, carting around grandchildren, and only being allowed one phone call a week!

Your problem is the problem that lots of us have, having been born into this privileged generation in the well-off section of the planet at just the right time. We look with horror on the idea of renouncing some pleasures.

We don't consider all the opportunity our rights afford us, rights that until very recently would have been unimaginable (and for a large section of our fellow human beings in other parts of the world are still unthinkable).

We are submerged in material goods—I'll spare you a sermon on our selfish and perverse abuse of globalization, which allows us to buy just about anything even if it is of dreadful quality. That little top? Check it online. It's there today but may be gone tomorrow.

Compare that to our parents' generation. My mom's silk gown has survived to this day despite me and my washing machine's best efforts. I accept that I don't go to that many formal receptions at which people would comment on its cut, but believe me, it makes me stand out from the crowd at morning Mass when a good 35 years separate me from the rest of the congregation of 12 elderly ladies all around me. I feel like a fashion model!

But it's not only giving up material possessions in every imaginable size and color that seem so necessary for our well-being that is hard for our generation. We also find it hard to give up other possibilities for our life. It's an adolescent thing—a period that will soon hit my own children but that I recall very well in my own life. A time when you want to live every possible life, experience everything, be everywhere, listen, read, know, and inhale all the possibilities life has to offer. And the idea that at some point you will have to choose one of these options and close the door on all the others seemed the closest thing to death itself for a 16-year-old.

And yet, despite all that, as my friend Francesco and I agreed one time after discussing such things for hours and hours in the car, no matter what you choose, what you become, what you do in life, you can only ever occupy the few inches your two feet cover (my size tens cover more than most).

That thought took away a lot of the existential angst. What will we become? What will we do in life? It didn't matter, we agreed. Even the most *bulo* person (Perugia slang for someone who makes a success of himself) has only two feet and can only be in one place at a time. In that way, the young Francesco and I—I wonder where he is now?—made a major step forward compared to most of the "overforties" I see all around me.

You, Agata, have everything. You are gifted in so many ways, but even you can only cultivate some of those gifts. You have to choose which ones. You have to make some decisions about your life, too. You have to decide on the man you want to spend the rest of your life with.

It's not easy, I know. Indeed, I know this truth only too well. My husband's most frequently uttered phrase (after "I'm tired"—poor soul, he gets home from work often in the middle of the night and nobody notices the next morning) is "Costanza, you can't do everything in this life."

Our lives, when all is said and done, will be the sum total of all the choices we have made over the years. What we choose to take and what we choose to leave behind.

Nowadays everyone seems to be desperate to keep all options open. I call it the emergency exit syndrome. What they don't realize is that the choice to leave something open necessarily requires closing off some other possibility. Refusing to decide closes off the possibility of following a path that leads to depths of emotion and riches of spirit that the world has never known. Experiencing an array of different love affairs won't teach you as much about love as living a single experience of love in all its depth.

That choice of a profound and lasting love will help you embrace your everyday life without searching out new emotions and sensations. It will help you love your life, which from the outside may seem very "normal." The path will lead you, through everyday life, up a slope that may be steep. But at the top, a great valley will open out before you—a hidden and secret place that the back lanes of "feelings" can never reach. It is experienced by very few . . .

I have to confess, I find it hard to practice what I preach. I hate making choices. I find it hard even to choose a table in the cafeteria and so always go to the end of the line (while secretly hoping that no one in front of me will take the last pear crumble).

Luckily, I have a husband endowed with industrial quantities of good sense and four children who reduce my available time for self-questioning to about eight minutes a day. Just long enough to say to myself, "What will I do now?" Generally, I spend the time gazing with discomfort at the shelf full of beauty products, working out how much money I've wasted on them, and remembering how many beauty regimes I have disregarded. Thankfully, Dior Capture skincare has done wonders for the complexion of Tetenno the Bunny, who now has a flawless line-free cloth face. With thoughts such as this, my eight minutes are up, and I have no decisions to make other than to embrace my life with new conviction.

You need to embrace life, too, choose one life and hold onto it tight. And decide on one man, too—just one. Men are a funny breed, but if you have space—it's useful to have a garden or at least a balcony—you can keep them in the home, and they will make good companions. I'd go for Paolo; why not marry him and have a family? It's time to act. Then if you want, you can give me a call and tell me about all his defects. You must excuse me if I have to put down the receiver every so often to prepare the lasagna while we speak. The main thing is that you will finally have made your decision. And from that moment on, your new life will begin.

A kiss from a devoted disciple of your style and taste, who can't wait to admire your choice of wedding dress,
C

I want to avoid clichés like "the right person will arrive when you are least expecting it," and I will also refrain from adding,

"And you will be out when they call." I should close this chapter here, having nothing more intelligent to add. I am sure I could find appropriate citations from millions of books, songs, and films. Marvelous words about meeting the right person. I would if I could, but alas, at the moment the only reflections that come to mind are those of Carrie Bradshaw from *Sex and the City*.

Despite the poverty of my cultural references, though, I feel I can't help myself saying something, even though, in doing so, I know I am entering a minefield. Here goes!

I am surrounded by lonely people, and thanks to the "village grandma" in me, I would love to see them settle down once and for all with the right person. In all honesty, though, I have to confess that not once have I ever succeeded in matchmaking a couple from among my circle of acquaintances. I suspect I will never be put in charge of the advice column—the one that my colleagues and I secretly read every morning first thing while pretending to be flicking through the financial journals.

When I propose inviting to dinner two unsuspecting candidates, my husband is adamant: "Leave them alone—they are fine as they are." He is clearly not moved by their tragic circumstances—free to go to the movies every evening with a different person, no school meetings to attend, no sleepless nights worrying about a child who has had a bump on the head . . . you know the routine: "Wake him every two hours to make sure he is responding properly, ma'am."

And who, I wonder, is going to wake me to check that I am still responding?

In my secret little archive of people I want to see married, there are some for whom even I am beginning to give up hope. These are people who have grown up and with age have lost that little bit of recklessness that is needed in life; they have become rigid and are now prisoners of their own routines. One colleague once told me about her morning ritual, a series of small sacred steps that could not be amended in any way, lasting two hours from the alarm clock going off to her leaving the house. For a mother on the other hand, the only certainty in the morning is that at some point I will manage to brush my teeth.

Yet I continue to believe that even my colleague will one day find something—or rather someone—even more interesting than her comfortable bed, or maybe it will be another person whose habits perfectly match her own.

The couple relationship corresponds to one of our deepest needs. Each of us exists in relationship with other people. Woman needs man and vice versa, each needs the other to fully discover his or her own identity. When women realize that they cannot find total fulfillment on their own, they resist the temptation of independence and offer themselves so as to receive in turn all that the other person can give. A man is unable to resist a woman who listens to his voice, who follows him, obeys him, and is supportive of him. We have to trust. We have to run the risk of getting it wrong if we want to achieve anything.

Certainly, the risk is enormous. To give one's self to another forever is no small step. Especially when there is no guarantee—no test, no insurance policy, nothing. You have to throw yourself into it without a safety net, and, if truth be told, it is a hard and crazy path to follow. It is a risk that you decide to take when you are mature and have learned to love yourself. It's only then that you are capable of such a gratuitous decision.

Many people my age don't get married because, while once it was the standard thing to do, maybe even the only thing to do, now it is just one of several possibilities. And we imagine that we will always be able to choose it at some point in the future as we now live life as an eternal adolescence. And it is also true that for many years, women, like men many years before them, have realized that they do not need to be married to have a decent sex life. So being beautiful, intelligent, educated, and professional can end up complicating things. It can cause us to fall into the trap of giving too much emphasis to our own autonomy, so that the idea of renunciation of self even in part becomes unthinkable.

As for men, whether we like it or not, it works like this: He is basically happy if he feels himself free. If he feels caged, oppressed, warned, and told off, he tries to worm out of the relationship. I can say this because I am an inveterate scolder, and when I am on a roll, I can see my husband rolling his eyes. I can see him thinking, "If I were to be asked right now 'where would you rather be?' I think the answer 'with my wife' would come just below the answer 'on a senior tour along the Amalfi Coast with free demonstrations of pots and pans and a complimentary pot holder.' Maybe preference number 24,726."

This idea that women somehow have the notion of obedience written into them—while man has a vocation to liberty and direction—is not pleasing to hear. But we have to try to examine it.

I believe that in the end, both in our own personal history and in the history of the world (because history has a beginning but also an end), the concepts of obedience and command will be overcome. At the moment, however, obedience is a necessary consequence of humanity's wounded nature, of original sin. It is through the patient daily practice of obedience that each of us can reach out to others and control our own egotism. Sometimes, in doing so, we will be comforted by both our senses and our emotions while at other times we have to go against them.

Love is essentially a choice; it's a decision—it has to do with emotions, but the emotional side is only one aspect of love. The current understanding of love inverts the hierarchy of values, placing feelings on top. Films and books are full of it. They are seas rippling with emotion; a gentle breeze passes over them but does not go deep. Sometimes our love that we believe to be noble and generous is in fact cowardly and egotistical. It's as trustworthy as our feelings, and that's not very trustworthy at all. "For you, darling, I would cross deserts and forests, passing through tempests and the darkest nights. Bye, then. I'll see you at eight o'clock in town. As long as it doesn't rain."

When we get married, the problem of no longer functioning purely on an emotional level arises, and that discovery is dramatic. If we get distracted, the other person becomes about as emotionally fulfilling as a dirty diaper, a pile of bills, or the smell of boiled cabbage. In my personal program, "Don't Get Distracted, Keep Being Good Company for Your Partner," one of the first points is to learn to speak the language of the other person.

Americans, as we all know, are a very precise people—so much so that when you go through US Customs, they politely ask you, "Excuse me, ma'am, are you planning to carry out any criminal or immoral activities during your stay?" That precision extends to dividing the language of love into five possible categories, an idea that, though so very American, has a lot to be said for it. For our actions to be meaningful to another person, that person has to understand them.

There are some people who, if they don't receive the gift of a "thing," a concrete, tangible object, they don't feel loved. This applies to two of my children. You can spend a great day with them showering them with affection, talking to them, and covering them with hugs and kisses, but if they don't get a present, if they don't get to unwrap a package, the day will have been no fun at all.

There are others who want time on their own with you, special moments dedicated only to them. One of my other children is like this. You could give him, let's say, the guitar he's always wanted or the latest PlayStation game, and you'll find that two seconds later, he trips over them as he comes to you wanting to talk, asking for your attention and needing to be listened to. With children like this, you save a lot of money. But it all has to be reinvested in cough drops or earplugs if you're really tired.

According to American author Gary Chapman (who came up with these distinctions), there are also some people who understand affection only through physical contact: kisses, embraces, caresses, those things that are always necessary in early childhood but that for most people become accessories in adulthood. I confess I distributed such kisses in industrial quantities when my children were babies, enough to give my lips a cramp. Nowadays, ordinary gestures of affection keep three of my children happy while one daughter still needs frequent physical contact—preferably with my neck!

As for me and my husband, alas, we also speak different languages—the two that are left. He speaks through acts of service, whereas I prefer words (I say this just in case any of my family, friends, and acquaintances might be in any doubt. So please, don't bother telling me the truth—compliments only, please!).

My husband, to try to express his affection, turns himself into a kind of Mr. Wolf—the problem solver from *Pulp Fiction*. He solves problems. I think there's a Mr. Wolf hidden inside every man. He has been trained through years of working in television, where it can often happen that everything breaks down a minute before air time. Something usually happens and all seems lost. Then someone manages to get the problem fixed and pulls out stops that no one even knew existed. I don't know how they do it. Maybe they use an old sock to adjust a malfunctioning machine or find some metal wire in their pocket to replace the circuits. Seeing the courageous professionalism and the classic Italian ingenuity of my colleagues always reassures me that nothing really terrible will happen to our country while they're around.

But I would much prefer my own personal Mr. Wolf to make some staggering declaration of love to me, words chosen to sweep me off my feet. (If I really let myself dream, they might even be accompanied by a bunch of roses, peonies, or even buttercups. I like lavender, too!)

But I fear he doesn't know how to say those words. He prefers to play with my affections using cables and hi-tech gadgets. "How beautiful is this?" he says to me triumphantly as though he were giving me a magnificent diamond ring. "Now we can show a video on our home computer while we record from somewhere else!" I suppose this possibility may prove useful in the unlikely event that our children—ages 3 to 11—unexpectedly taking off, all four of them, for a short vacation visiting the château of the Loire Valley.

I remember in the early years of our marriage, I found it hard to understand why he didn't appreciate the magnificent letter I had written him, though doing so had meant neglecting those bourgeois boring tasks like preparing dinner. I always got the impression that he would rather have eaten than read!

"You never tell me how much you care about me," I lament.

"What do you mean I don't care? I went to get you that Diet Coke you wanted in the middle of the night from the 24-hour drug store!" Diet Coke is an essential item in our home.

Am I allowed to stray off the point for a moment? Am I allowed to do a bit of product placement in the middle of this book? I just wanted to let any marketing directors reading this book know what kind of comforts I crave daily. So in no particular order, there's the newspaper *Il Foglio*, Giorgio Beverly Hills perfume (it's not my fault that I was an adolescent in the eighties!), the whole range of Sisley crèmes, and Diet Coke or Coca-Cola Zero (preferably cherry flavor, though unfortunately that particular wonder is not sold on the Italian market). These are requirements for my very survival—as well as the presence of the Holy Spirit, but for that particular gift, it's the Top Man you need to turn to, not the head of marketing!

But enough of all that, where were we?

I remember. I was laying out my program of requirements for "Don't Get Distracted, Keep Being Good Company for Your Partner."

So first, try to speak the language of your spouse. Next on the list, I would recommend to find your own space. I think this is important right from the very start of the relationship when there's a tendency for symbiosis, but it's even more necessary when children arrive. You need your own space to recharge your battery or, to use another analogy, to fill up the gas tank to be able to keep going on and on and on for the family.

Obviously, this "me time" can't be at the expense of the relationship. (It wouldn't be a great idea to be spending all your time with the guy who's your closest friend on the basis that he "understands" you.) That's just common sense. (Similarly, it's no good spending three hours a day training for a marathon run because it "makes me feel good" while leaving all of four minutes to be "fully available" to your offspring.)

This might seem an obvious thing to say, and I'm glad if that's the way it strikes you, dear reader, but I meet many people (if I'm being honest, mostly women) who find it hard to set aside any time for themselves, the result being that they are constantly tired and moaning. Sometimes, going home half an hour later can be a loving gesture if creating that space allows you to recharge your batteries. We all need to give ourselves little gifts of time alone. One thing that's definitely to be recommended—if it can be done without laying extra weight on the shoulders of someone else in the family—is to have a long lie on a Sunday morning (which should be possible on the one occasion every two years or so when the children don't wake up at seven o'clock in the morning.).

Personally, even during the most hectic periods of my life, when I was breastfeeding a baby a couple of days old and at the same time trying to deal with a flu outbreak infecting the whole family, I always tried to keep open a narrow path of communication with myself. Every morning at Mass, I complain to the Boss about all the things that have gone wrong, and we have a friendly chat about the various solutions (I know I should be spending more time giving thanks, but He is very good and never takes offense).

And I always try to find a way to fit in some time for my favorite sport—running. Sometimes doing so requires real imagination and effort. I've been running since I was twelve, a time when the word *fitness* didn't exist in Italian; gyms were huge, dark, smelly rooms on the ground floor of school buildings; and the phrase "body mass index" was the stuff of science fiction. Running was, and is, for me, pure passion—a joyful celebration of the human body. You can start running when you are half-dead with tiredness or when you're furious with three or even all four children at the same time, but you return with all forgotten.

Three Years Later . . .

Agata did get married, obviously (do I even have to say that?), but not to Paolo, who was the guy I was hoping for. The main thing is that she chose one man and chose him forever.

I don't have to tell you that the ceremony, the dress, and, I imagine, the family reception were fabulous. As was the party one day later for friends, which took place in one of Rome's most elegant gardens. It was so elegant, in fact, that I'd never heard of it, perhaps because it had no swings, no Ukrainian babysitters, and no kiosks selling artificially colored popsicles.

Agata remains my style icon, effortlessly elegant, laid back inside but able to switch to Germanic efficiency when necessary. I had given up hope of ever seeing the day. Taking on a commitment that is not merely provisional is the one thing that repels our generation. We want to look ahead but always keeping one eye on the emergency exit, not realizing that committing our whole life to something greater than ourselves renders us better people.

My friend has finally chosen to follow one, definitive, clear path. No longer is she dominated by the stress of having to take every opportunity that presents itself, of always having to look over her shoulder, of always networking. She has made her choice and so far, she doesn't seem to be looking back. That's quite the achievement for someone who previously agonized if she booked a holiday in Mexico for fear that a better offer might turn up, so much so that clicking the "Purchase Ticket" link was a major anxiety.

This is probably not the right moment to say so, but I have a confession of my own to make: I don't know how to use a credit card online. In fact, the very idea fills me with panic. Maybe it's because I'm subhuman—I must be, since I never pass the CAPTCHA Test, which is used by online retailers to confirm that they are indeed dealing with a human being.

What Agata did, putting her whole life on the line without any plan B, is ironically something that provides us with great inner peace. I get piles of letters from people asking me, "Do you think he—she—is the right person?" Obviously, I can't answer that question, but perhaps that is not the most important thing. What really matters is that decision to commit oneself, to put our liberty on the line. That is a true act of freedom. God is not a sadistic quiz show host looking down on us to see if we have guessed the winning number. "I am sorry, ma'am, the correct answer was 3." It's for us to decide on a path and follow it as far as it goes. Whether it was the right path or not we'll discover at the end.

Or perhaps afterward.

Chapter 5

Margherita

Or

To Hold up the World, You Have to Be below It

Dear Margherita,

I had intended to come to your wedding with a beautiful letter for you. After all, I am the bridesmaid, and my name will be near the top of the closing credits. It seemed only right that I should show up properly prepared.

Better prepared, I should add, than I was for my own big day, at which I was certainly ready spiritually, but not as perfectly made up as I should have been, apart from a white eye shadow that my sister forced me to buy—I was running late because I had gone out for a jog two hours before the ceremony. I remember I was also struck down by an insane desire to laugh, which meant that I didn't come out too well in the wedding photographs Uncle Gianfranco took.

But back to your big day . . . I salute you for one thing: You managed to get my husband Guido to wear a tie, which is no mean feat. "Why is Dad wearing that funny little scarf thing around his neck?" Lavinia asked, clearly bemused at the rarely used garment. I'm sorry that the rest of us were so stylistically challenged at the fairytale event that was your wedding. I confess, I didn't get around to writing to you beforehand, nor did I manage to dress up myself and my children as elegantly as I had hoped. (Why is it they always seem to have a new chocolate stain on their shirt, a shoelace untied, trousers that are either too short or too long, or tights with a hole in them from which a skinned knee peers out?)

Never mind. Disheveled as always, all six of us made it—on time too—which was just as well since I was required to sit next to you. It was a celebration that was filled with divine grace and precious moments, even if my daughters remember it most of all for the lace train of your wedding dress, which not even Cinderella, our absolute style icon, could hope to match. Since then, I've often heard them say to each other, "This will be useful for when my prince comes to marry me," as they divide up among themselves plastic earrings and toy diamonds.

The boys remember it, I'm afraid, as the dreadful day that the Roma soccer team lost to Genoa's Sampdoria and thus missed out on the Italian Soccer Championship. What can I say? They are males—the entry-level model. They are not absolute rednecks, though. Bernardo is a model student, never gets less than an A at school and seems like a little soldier, always ready to carry out his orders. Tommaso, who is a little less ordered (and is known at home as the pigsty boy), called me one night last year to ask me when the Tehran Conference was held—an event about which I was blissfully ignorant, given that the last historical event to stick in my mind was the collapse of the Roman Empire.

A few evenings ago, he said, "Mom, what is dialectical materialism?" My answer? "If you don't get to sleep now, I'm going to call Dad." This pathetic attempt to frighten the boy was delivered while I frantically looked up the philosophy section of the encyclopedia or the history book that I have learned to keep constantly at hand, along with other fundamentals such as the box set of the *West Wing* or the novena to Our Lady of Good Hope. Such items are essential when I realize, as Ennio Flaiano, the screenwriter, pithily put it, "There are no gaps in my ignorance." What a boy! If I catch him on the computer without permission, he's more likely to be learning about the Visigoths than playing a game of Texas hold 'em.

But belonging to the male gender, he too has a defect that is almost universal among men. His brain goes to mush when he sees a moving ball. I know men, ordinary men—and even extraordinary ones like the one I married—who, when they hear the opening whistle of a sports game, switch over from the action movies of Sam Peckinpah to the *Signora in Giallorosso* soccer show. They put down Dostoyevsky's *The Idiot* and listen in to some local radio show for the hard of thinking. Such is the desire to hear the sports news—they feel no shame!

I'm only telling you this to prepare you, given that you have taken on one of this species, and not just for a weekend away, but for your whole life, until death do you part.

For that reason, I wanted to tell you about the real gift of marriage—much more important than my official wedding present, which I hope arrived on time. It's the secret of a holy marriage, which is another way of saying a happy marriage.

The secret is this: Women need to take a step back from the man they have chosen. You know me well enough to know that such an idea doesn't come easily. I made my own the motto from my grandfather (the colonel): "Wall or no wall, advance three steps forward!"

For example, I think I may be the subject of one of only seven or eight cases in the whole world of a runner crashing into a car. As for the damage? I was left with concussion and the car with a major dent. I wish I could spice the story up a little, but alas it wasn't an Aston Martin I collided with, just a Fiat Punto. My point is this: I'm not someone who gives in easily. I had to learn that skill. I did it, I hope and believe, because I think a bride needs to be welcoming above and beyond any other qualities she may have.

You know how I hate losing—as we all do. I was always ultracompetitive at school and college. Even more so on the sports field, sport being the only "rest" that I allowed myself in the years between early adolescence and my last pregnancy. Many is the time I would go for a 15-mile run with my head full of Homer and Aeschylus just to clarify my thoughts.

In the years when the two if us were out of touch, I used to prepare myself for marathons by going out for a run at three o'clock in the morning, even though I had to be in the studios at five o'clock for the early morning news show. I used to go out in shorts in a city I didn't know (I was new to Rome then) in the dark, and it all seemed quite normal to me; even when, on one occasion, I came across a madman, completely naked in front of the Victor Emmanuel Monument in the center of Rome in the middle of the night. I suspect when he saw me, he asked himself who on earth was this crazy woman running by!

And even now that I am a lady on the cusp of her forties (I have no time for that "girl" stuff when we are talking about fortysomethings!), I run when I can, not training for a specific event, but when someone over-takes me—even if it's just a pigeon—it sure fires up that old competitive gene again.

But back to the life of the couple. With your partner you have to compete in the opposite direction: Wall or no wall, take three steps back, not forward! And you have to do it even if you don't understand his reasons for wanting to do something, even when you are con-vinced you are right. At that moment, make an act of faith in your husband. Don't follow the world's logic—that understandable desire to be right—but rather fol-low God's logic. It's God who put your husband at your side, that saintly man who puts up with you despite everything, and who, incidentally, is a handsome guy. And if something he does really annoys you, take it up with God first. Get down on your knees, and in most cases, you'll find the problem gets resolved.

Luigi is the means God has chosen to love you, and he is your pathway to heaven. So when he says something, try to see it as though God himself was speaking to you—though obviously with due discernment and wisdom and intelligence. Obviously, you can't take everything he says in that way—he is human, after all—but nevertheless, he does sometimes see things much more clearly than you.

Our vocation, whatever it is in life, is essentially to make each other happy. As Pavel Evdokimov, the Russian Orthodox theologian puts it, if the objective end of marriage is to generate children, the subjective end is to generate ourselves.

Without Luigi, Margherita cannot fully be herself. Do you realize what a priceless gift you have on your hands? In this task, with God's help, you will regenerate yourself.

"But how?" you asked a thousand times in our telephone chats. "Do I have to pretend he's right even when he's not?" I would say yes. First because it may be your limited viewpoint that makes you think he is wrong. And if he is the means to your full self-realization, your development as a person, it's precisely when you think differently about things that you should open yourself to him and welcome him.

In those moments his words should have a special significance for you. They are precious because they add something to you, they complete you in a way, they help you grow and set out on a new path. If you accept only that which is in line with your own way of thinking and way of acting, you're not really married to a man but to yourself.

So try to submit to him. When you have to choose between what you prefer and what he prefers, go for his choice. It's not difficult. When you have to decide, and you have weighed the arguments for and against, and when the answer still doesn't seem all that clear, let him have the last word. This is a bit harder, I grant you. And when it comes to a situation where you both have clear opinions, and it seems clear to you that his is wrong, for your sake and also for the children's sake, trust his lucidity. I know this can seem an impossible challenge. It can actually make you afraid, because abandoning one's own opinions can be frightening. But remember this: You are not throwing yourself into a void. You are throwing yourself into his arms.

Nice words, aren't they? On reading them, you would think that I was an angelic creature. The truth is I have only heard and read nice words. Putting them into practice is another matter, and I'm not sure how I'm doing on that score. I certainly don't succeed every time and in every circumstance.

Out of interest, I asked my husband to cast an eye over what I've just written and the good news is that he didn't respond to it with loud and vehement protests. No raspberries blown and no grunts, which would signal that he doubted my sincerity. That's something! In fact, the idea of submission being elevated to a scientific theory was one he seemed to like. "Hey, dearest one, are you finished in the John?" he asked me the other night. Being a Roman, he manages to eliminate any poetry from our lyrical exchanges.

You'll see, I assure you, that a man cannot refuse a woman who respects him, who recognizes his authority, who loyally tries to listen to him, who puts aside her own way of seeing things, who bites her tongue, who is always ready to have a joke, who is ready to laugh at the absurdities in life and to play down his weaknesses (we are not all good at this), and who is willing for the sake of love to strike out on a different path to the one she would have chosen for herself.

Little by little you will notice that he begins to ask you what you think, what he should do, and in which direction the family should go. It's a case of respect being won through respect being shown through submission. So it is that, having finally gained my partner's respect, I feel able to explain to him—calmly—what a great advantage it would be for our household if I could have a walk-in closet in our bedroom. The first benefit would be that I would no longer have a pile of black tops lying on the floor lost to the human eye, and so would not buy seven new ones in the mistaken belief that the first lot were gone forever.

And even when the good fruits seem to be taking their time in appearing (apparently I am not getting the walk-in closet), we Christians have to be confident that they are still maturing. We are supposed to be filled with joy and hope, aren't we? We know that whatever happens to us can't be measured according to the values of the world. We know that every suffering, even the small ones—you don't agree with him, you wouldn't have made that plan, you wouldn't have chosen that holiday or that night out—if it is accepted with love, produces good fruits.

Sometimes they may be hidden, but the effort is not in vain. "May whatever causes you to suffer be more precious to you than the hermitage is to me." Thus spoke St. Francis of Assisi, who would have loved to spend every minute in his isolated hermit's hut in sweet and endless prayer but chose instead to be among ordinary people and live with his followers, who sometimes didn't understand him.

Remember, we are not interested in mortification per se or austerity for its own sake. We can happily talk about spiritual classics such as *The Interior Castle* while in the same breath discussing the latest shade of Chanel nail polish, the impossible to find *vernis riva*. We can read the *Dialogue of Divine Providence* and then find ourselves gossiping—quite disgraceful, I know—about Carla Bruni's only known physical defect, a shortish neck (there is justice in the world after all!).

We practice mortification only for a greater good, and this good is about welcoming your husband and, in doing so, generating a new you.

I have to say—and please don't be offended by this—that when you tell me how he makes you angry, it always seems to me to be about silly little things. Little pinpricks to your pride, little attacks on your weak self-esteem. When you realize who you are and what you are worth (a very great deal, believe me; I know you and I care for you), you shouldn't be worried by the odd criticism. OK, so you are not an expert cook or a perfect homemaker. Is it a problem if I say that to you? If he says it to you, just tell him he's right and that you are working on it. Seeing your sweetness and humility and your efforts to improve, he too will change. No sermon required; he will change because he sees his reflection in you.

You may find yourself thinking that it's taking forever. That Luigi is never going to change, that you're involved in a series of transactions that never seem to balance out. But that's not so. No loving act or gesture goes to waste. The step back that you may take will be transformed into two steps forward for you as a couple. No bitter word left unspoken will be a cause for regret.

It's a hard path, exhausting even. You'll feel like you are the one doing all the giving. We are good at playing the victim card; in a millisecond, we're back in the 1950s, dressed as downtrodden housewives, all flared skirts and perms. But is that really true? Are you really the one doing all the giving? He is probably thinking something similar—that he has to walk that extra mile to please you.

My sense is that we shouldn't play that game of who gives most in a relationship. The relationship works when the person who is able to gives most. You may feel a martyr at this precise moment, but throughout life the balance shifts back and forth.

Another thing is this: You think you love him as he wants to be loved when in fact you love him in the way that suits you best. You are forever leaving him little notes whereas he would rather you did something practical for him—like inviting your mother-in-law over for dinner, for example! You want him to bring you bunches of flowers whereas he shows he loves you by going to the pizzeria to get you your favorite topping of octopus and tomato. If you speak his language—the language of practical gestures—he will learn to speak yours, the language of declarations of love delivered from a kneeling position to the sound of romantic violins.

You complain that he doesn't speak very much at all. But where have you been living all these years? Have you never noticed that most men make declarations only when they wish to impart information that is both useful and pertinent. It's taken me a few years, but I now realize that there's no point in trying to engage my husband in conversation about such topics as the sentimental needs of human beings. If I really need to talk to him, all I need to do is express a decisive (though probably mistaken) view on the 4-2-3-1 formation of the Roma soccer team or the war in Afghanistan, and you can be sure that an answer will be forthcoming.

There's always got to be that constant give and take, and sometimes, when we get too caught up in ourselves, we feel as though we are giving too much and getting too little in return.

For example, if it were up to me, our house would always be full of people. But my husband, rather than share his evening with others—and, in doing so, double his enjoyment—would prefer the option of migrating to a forest to be on his own. In cases like this, it's hard to strike a balance, so it requires a degree of tolerance on both sides. It's hard to judge who gives way more, especially since, over the years we have had to pull up four new seats at the table—now permanently occupied by little people who are there every day for lunch and dinner.

When in doubt, though, do what he asks. Submit with an act of faith.

With me, to give you another example, everything is planned so that I can fit in as many tasks as possible in my day. I am a bit like Flipper the dolphin—the more hoops I jump through the more points I get in my own mind.

For my husband, on the other hand, good ideas emerge from boredom. They come out of the void, and I have to say they sometimes work out. It only works though if we have three hours with absolutely nothing to do. We may all go for an unplanned trip to the movies to see Charlie Chaplin's *Limelight*, visit the underground levels of the Basilica of San Clemente in Rome, or get involved in a never-ending ball game, which would involve the three females of the family too. Every so often we abandon the pitch to collect flowers or invent a new game, though the old favorite Truth or Dare is always the most popular. But I have to say that every now and again, planning has its advantages when you have to keep track of appointments with the pediatrician and dentist, children's parties, homework, little friends visiting to play, catechism classes, and sports tournaments, but I am learning to be a bit more flexible, the supreme quality of every wife and mother.

That flexibility will become even more important in your life soon when your capacity for welcoming will be shown not only toward your husband but also toward your children. Their well-being and happiness will be determined at least partly—and at least until they grow up (Good Lord how many years will that be?)—by your capacity to absorb their bad moods, tantrums, tiredness, and grumpiness.

I don't know why, but it seems a privilege reserved especially for parents—children always behave worse with us. Everyone knows that. I suppose it's the same with adults. Don't we tend to let off steam with those that we know care for us, no matter what? With whom do we feel comfortable enough to let our masks slip, to let ourselves go and reveal our full repertoire of ugly traits? Only with those we know will never abandon us (e.g., your mom or your best friend from high school—in your case, that's me!). "Listen, I have to rant a bit . . ." Both of us know that when the phone call starts like this, the person at the other end of the line is required only to listen, to nod vigorously, to share the pain in a convincing manner, to admire in an over-the-top way, and to absolutely *never* give intelligent advice. Because at such times we don't want a solution. We only want a hearty nonverbal pat on the back.

Children seem to learn this lesson that we will always be there for them. From about three minutes into life, they understand that. That means that every uncomfortably full diaper, every candy they are not allowed to eat, every homework challenge—depending on their age—leads invariably to their letting loose on us through tantrums, long faces, tears, and various insults (recently, I was told that I was acting like a "fascist colonel"). In response and to get away, I have tried in the past saying things like "Kids, I am off to buy a packet of cigarettes," but no one believes me. Maybe because I don't smoke.

I predict that before long, Luigi too will take advantage of your soft cuddly nature—even if you weigh less than eight pounds, you are still soft and cuddly inside—to fire off his displeasure at some annoyance or other that bedevils human existence and that by some mysterious path can be traced back to you.

Don't worry, it means nothing and soon passes. Try to be welcoming in moments such as this. He may not actually want a solution to his problems, but try to encourage him, tell him that you appreciate what he is doing, and—if I can use my own husband as an example of the male species—allow him to retreat like a caveman into his cave, which nowadays may assume the high-tech form of a computer screen. The need is the same—a kind of primeval haven.

When that happens, don't moan. Call me or another female friend. Warn us right away not to take you too seriously, and then you can complain your head off! Don't do this with him, because a man—why, I don't know, you would need to speak to a psychiatrist, a philosopher, or a "maniatrist" of some description—when faced with your complaints, tries to find some practical solution. He may suggest lengthening the childcare or taking a vacation, when all you really want is for him to say that all is well, that you are a hero, that he admires you, and that you are one of a kind.

And don't—I know you too well—start asking yourself if you made the wrong choice, if he really was the man for you. The devil—the origin of whose name is *dià-ballo*, meaning "divide"—uses this trick to get his way. He wants to divide. He wants to divide us from ourselves, from God, and from the person to whom we have sworn to be faithful.

It's not you who has made a mistake, nor is it him. It's simply that welcoming is our particular charisma, while guiding and sustaining is theirs.

I don't think it's all about cultural conditioning—we would have to ask the aforementioned "maniatrist." But my experience suggests otherwise.

I have a very dear friend who lives in Germany. She's a genius; she has an amazing brain. I hadn't heard from her for a while, and every now and again, I would imagine her life, so different from my own. She and her partner with interchangeable roles . . . him pushing the stroller, her going to the briefing or planning meeting. I called her on her birthday only to discover that she had decided to stay at home and live the life of a full-time mom, leaving her degree in electrical engineering on the shelf for a while. We ended up chatting and sharing news about every aspect of family dynamics—her family and those of her German friends whom I envy as they seem to spend their mornings drinking tea and their afternoons visiting parks that I imagine are tidier than my living room. And despite the fact that we live in such different cultures (in hers, the streets are clean and the baby stroller parking spaces are actually left for parents who have babies!), we found that there were almost no significant differences between us.

Dear Margherita, what else can I say to you? I promise that I will keep an eye out for you and your happiness, which you have to start building from now on, even though there are more powerful guardian angels I could suggest for you. Remember, I am only a few years ahead of you down this road, and I always make the same mistakes. You can pay me back by telling the story to my girls of the handsome prince who carries you off to his castle. Even if he needs a little help with his timekeeping . . .

Your bridesmaid who sends you a kiss and promises to keep cheering you both on,
C

I never imagined that I would come to reconsider the endless sermons that were preached to us without warning by Signora Ciotola (her name translates as "Mrs. Bowl," and that is indeed her real name and not a name given to her on account of her ample girth). Nor did I ever imagine that I would come to value the pearls of wisdom imparted by the old ladies who used to go for a walk in the shade on hot summer evenings with my grandmother. For us flirty girls, still coming to terms with our first attempts at makeup, with our straps "accidentally" having slipped off our shoulders, we didn't have to do much to earn their disapproval. A flash of shoulder was enough to bring on looks of disgust and loud sighs, which didn't augur well for our destiny. The model woman that they discussed in their conversations—strong and silent, at the heart of the family like the hub controlling the spokes of a wheel—seemed less plausible to me than Sigourney Weaver playing Ripley in the film *Alien* (I am a 1980s girl!). I couldn't look after myself. What chance did I have of looking after someone else?

But then you grow up and you learn to try your best. I'm only sorry that neither of my two grandmas lived long enough to see all four of my children, so far growing up a bit muddy here and there but basically unscathed without too many stitches! Grandma Gina would still have had something to say, though, given that I have forgotten how to crochet and I could do better at managing the household budget. My son Bernard once told one of his friends, "My mom is very good at heating up frozen food," in an attempt to persuade the little boy to stay for dinner!

But I'm sure their grandmas would have approved of the children's report cards and their piety. My daughter Livia once said to me that when she grows up, she wants to be a saint—"Saint Teresa of Dalila." I think she meant Avila!

I often think of those women of past generations when I see women of my own generation in search of their identity and suffering because of it. The women of yesteryear didn't have to look too far for a role in life. Life had assigned them a very clear one. It was a role that, in a way, protected them and made their search for identity less difficult. They didn't seem unhappy to me, and if they were, they kept it to themselves. If I had spoken to them about obedience, we would have understood each other.

Now though, there are very few of my Christian friends with whom I can discuss our ideas about marriage. If we speak about them to our "worldly" friends, they respond in one of three ways. They insult us, they feel sorry for us, or they suggest we seek psychological help as soon as possible. In a way, this is only to be expected.

The strange thing is that even among our fellow Christians, when you speak about submission, they think you are joking. "Sorry? What do you mean? I take it you are being ironic?"

There are few Christians who try every now and again to distance themselves from their culture—not the culture of St. Jerome and his Vulgate Bible but that culture that considers freedom, self-determination, and free will as ultimate, untouchable values in life. We should have known this would be the case; we were warned about it in the parables of the salt of the earth and the yeast in the bread.

To speak about submission provokes a reaction of disapproval, shock, rebellion, anger. Disgust, even. It's not only that original sin leaves in us a trace of hatred for the idea of obeying anyone other than ourselves; the culture of self-sufficiency in which we are all immersed—even Christians—affects us too, even though we are supposed to be people who have promised to serve others and put ourselves last.

St. Paul, in his letter to the Ephesians, explains how we should serve each other: "Wives, be submissive to your husbands, as is fitting in the Lord. The husband is the head of the wife just in so far as he is to her what Christ is to the Church. He gave his life for her. And so just as the Church submits to Christ so should wives to their husbands in all things" (Eph 5:22–24). Not even priests dare say such things these days for fear that we women will stone them to death!

Yet I have seen that for those who try out this advice, it is a path to salvation. It's not paradise—we hope for that in the life to come—but it's a kind of salvation here and now, in this life. In other words, it brings us peace, a full and satisfying married life.

It's a life that even nonbelievers should try out. Because, as St. Paul explains just a few verses later, "You husbands, love your wives as Christ loved the Church giving his life for her. . . . In this way husbands have the duty to love their wives as they love their own bodies, because he who loves his wife loves himself . . . for this reason a man shall leave his father and mother and will be joined to a woman and the two shall become one flesh" (Eph 5:25–31).

It may well be true that all happy families look the same— who am I to contradict Tolstoy? But I don't see a great variety in the unhappy ones either: betrayals, standoffs, trials of strength, subtle power plays, and invidious comparisons. ("I did more than you." "No, I did more." Time to call in the judge!)

As usual the only new contribution to the age-old debate comes from God. When we speak of submission—under our breath of course to avoid being lynched—we have to escape from the logic and language of the world that sees everything through the prism of power and domination. Our King reigns from the Cross, but in this way, He conquered the previously unconquerable enemy—death. That being so, we too have to throw off the logic of power—we have to completely overthrow it. First because submission is not the fruit of depression; we don't do it because we think we don't matter or are not worth anything. And then we must remember that the corollary of that choice on the part of the woman is the aforementioned willingness of the man to die for her.

When St. Paul exhorts women to be "below," he doesn't suggest for a moment that they are inferior. The opposite is true. It was Christianity that, for the first time in the history of the world, defended women's role and valued their dignity. The most wonderful creature ever to live was a woman, for starters! And let's not forget that Jesus scandalized his contemporaries in how he honored and interacted with women. It was to women that he first showed himself after the resurrection; who knows where the men were? At the soccer game, perhaps—given that it was a Sunday.

"That St. Peter was a total wimp before the Holy Spirit appeared to him," my son opined one day. His language might have been a bit colorful, but he was theologically correct.

The submission St. Paul talks about is a gift, freely given like every gift. If it weren't, it would be a burden instead. It's a gift of self that is spontaneous and made out of love. I renounce my egoism for your sake. And if we have to speak in terms of greatness and littleness, of strength and weakness, of power, then let's remember those words: "He who wishes to be first among you must become your servant." This is the measure of a person's greatness.

"Let he who has the most intelligence use it," my mother used to say to us when we were young. Her hope was that this noble call would plant within us seeds of goodness when we were planning to knock each other senseless for very good reasons, such as who got to choose the television channel or who got the new bike. For the record, the tactic never worked.

Women should not feel belittled by St. Paul's exhortation. The opposite is in fact true.

The trouble is that for many centuries and in many cultures, we were forced to be submissive. In Italian the word is *sottomesso*—literally "placed under." And this had nothing to do with the logic of self-giving, the gift of self for the beloved. Rather, it was a submission that was all about power and force—the world's logic, in other words. That's why to talk about "obedience" today still touches a raw nerve. Feminism, in a sense, has the merit of having brought a bit of justice into lives where there was precious little justice. (Alas, in many non-Christian cultures, there is still not much justice for women.) The only problem is that a certain kind of feminism gave the wrong answers and, in doing so, inadvertently brought about a lot of unhappiness. It has led to a new kind of slavery for women who think they are free and who, in fact, have missed the target.

"Your desire will be for your husband, and he will rule over you," Genesis says. There's a hidden spark here, a way to happiness. Right here, on this earth.

A woman is obedient because she listens, not because she considers herself worthless. The humble person knows his or her strengths and weaknesses. But while it's one thing to know these things, it's quite another to be reminded of them by another person. And so, dear children, I would ask you not to speak too loudly about the depressing repetitiveness of my cooking, and it's not strictly necessary to call me Princess Flatbelly in front of everyone!

When a woman places herself "under"—not so as to be trampled, but so as to support and welcome—she gives a positive example to her husband and to the whole family. The woman precedes the man who feels the need to be accepted.

With a wife like this, who is loyal and doesn't try to be some kind of rival, who doesn't try to control everything or dominate or play the "poor little woman" card, man is encouraged to be fruitful. The idea of having a baby won't seem quite so frightening, for one thing.

So it's about loving first but also loving last. It's our task to keep loving, to keep the flame of love burning in the family home. This is especially necessary at those moments when love—which is not only a feeling but first and foremost a commandment— requires a strong secure decision.

For example, it's a big decision not to betray in marriage when you yourself have been betrayed.

Can I just make clear that what follows is absolutely *not* for my husband's eyes, and the worthy words that follow apply to all marriages except my own!

So as I was saying, a woman who has been betrayed in love can defend her love even when it is in mortal danger by staying faithful and continuing to love. Such a situation is like being caught in a dreadful storm, but it needn't be a shipwreck. The vase may never look new again, but with a bit of glue, it can be repaired.

And who knows? It may be that broken and mended section that turns out to be the strongest part of the vase. It can be the new starting point for a relationship. In this way we women defend life, bearing its name high even when all seems lost.

To forgive doesn't mean to forget all that happened. It's not about refusing to face up to the pain we feel. It's not about trying to ignore the pain as though good and evil were indistinguishable. Rather, it's about putting the disorder to one side and helping the good to triumph over the bad.

Women who manage this are the strongest, most tenacious, and most loving women you will ever meet. They have broad shoulders, they are able to work the miracle that is required to overcome a betrayal, to tend the wound that is left and search once more for unity.

You can't say the same alas for men, because men and women love in different ways: women love with a specific kind of love that is able to appreciate its uniqueness. Men can be fragile and unable to distinguish the difference between themselves and women in their way of loving. It's only women who appear able to transmit hope, to stay strong and encourage others in situations of great pain, when the problem seems inextricable and desperate. But even when we're not talking about formal betrayal, putting the relationship in mortal danger, there are many other little betrayals that we may have to deal with.

Inevitably, there comes a time when habit takes some of the sheen off the relationship.

Even the wife of Robert Redford (not the wrinkled organizer of the Sundance Film Festival but the movie legend of *Butch Cassidy and the Sundance Kid* fame), on seeing him wander around the house in his underpants, wearing the wrong socks, clinging to the television remote control during a Lakers game, would feel tempted to give a second look to the good-looking young grocery store clerk from West Hollywood.

But even in circumstances like this, love functions if you value what is exclusive and permanent. You have to avoid following your emotions, your instincts, your desire to try out some new emotion and undiscovered sensation. Sometimes it strikes me how sad many of our books and films are today. So often they are a commentary on emptiness. They represent a boring repetition and demonstration of the fact that in following our ego, we feel ill and unsatisfied. We are like grains of wheat that resist falling on the ground. We are all good at saying, "I don't want to" or "I don't feel like it."

Pope John Paul II, when he used to go to summer camps with young people as a young priest, would offer this advice: "Don't say, 'I love you.' Say instead, 'I participate with you in the love of God.'" It's a completely different thing.

Three Years Later . . .

Technically, you would have to say that not everything worked out perfectly for Margherita and her husband Luigi (who could say that about their own marriage?). But given that while she reflects on the whole experience, she continues to produce children—three at the last count, if I'm not mistaken . . . I've taken her off my "most needy" list. She remains my dear friend (we have been close since high school), but now she's in a different section of my contacts book—the one under "Compatible with Low Levels of Neuron Activity." When she starts going on about how tired she is, I do with her what I do with myself: I only listen superficially, though this doesn't stop my kids taking advantage of my being on the phone to extort from me all sorts of subtle favors so that by the end of the call I discover I am the new owner of a Fireman Smurf toy. On other occasions, I discover that while I have been on the call, I have spent eye-watering amounts of money on pizzas or said yes to three school friends coming over to play.

Nowadays, though, Margherita's questions are easy to answer and tend to involve just small adjustments in her daily routine. Maggie, dear, you must realize by now that there's no point going on about him not being punctual. Put a microchip collar on the kids, or tattoo your number on his inner thigh and do a head count at the dinner table to make sure everybody is there! And stop asking him to take the kids to the park. I think if you stop trying to organize his time with the children, he'll want to do it himself.

Your doubts now are nothing compared to what they were in the past when it was always, "Is he Mr. Right?" and "What if I throw my lot in with him and somebody better comes along? Will he make me happy?"

Those questions posed by the "old Margherita," the one who hadn't learned to make room for another person in her life, are the same infantile and narcissistic concerns that I hear raised again and again by those thinking about getting married. They speak about love that is in fact possession, the possession of another person to make them feel better.

The love that Margherita is learning (and teaching me), on the other hand, is very different. It's a vision that sees love as a path to eternal life, because that's really the point of marriage—to generate new life (if it comes), but before that to generate ourselves, penetrating together that mystery of "male and female He created them in the image and likeness of God." The journey involves traveling with the other person, for the other person, and thanks to the other person, a path that can sometimes be tiring. It's tiring because it leads to the birth of something new. You are no longer two individuals but a communion of lives.

So if the "other" in the other person regenerates you, completes you in some way, then it should be welcomed with open arms—even if it makes you angry or nervous sometimes, even if it hurts you or you don't like it. The point is that in welcoming "the other" you are taking a step in the right direction.

To give you an example, Margherita would, if she could, have people over to dinner every night. Luigi on the other hand would quite happily carve out a solitary space for himself in a rock in Capadocia! She never stops talking. He, like certain other husbands I know, needs to be prodded every now and again to see if he is still alive. She likes to fold his socks using a ruler so as to have three straight rows in the second drawer on the left, while he has a rather more "flexible" approach to tidiness. For him the phrase "The house is tidy" means there are no children's bodies on the floor.

At a certain point, she gave in to the simple idea that they were just different. She decided to allow her husband to be himself. She realized that it wasn't up to her to decide how everyone else in the house should act. (This is an important lesson for the children to learn too.)

She has begun this work on herself, which is a bit like a house restoration but carried out on her own character, and she has been transformed from a carping baby to a marvelous welcoming woman. She still allows herself a monthly phone call to complain, but I think we should all be allowed that!

Chapter 6

Agnese

Or

Living with the Big Lebowski

Dear Agnese,

Luckily, you are one of us. A normal person.

"Those two must be just starting out," we said to each other as we watched you from our seat in the stalls of everyday life, which is always full of little annoying problems to solve. You know the sort of thing . . . seeing the plumber drive off in his shiny truck, leaving you with a bathroom that's out of order.

"I'll pop back tomorrow, lady. It's broke."

Yes, well, I could've told you that before you charged me for a wasted visit!

Life is always full of little issues that need dealing with: the measles knocking the kids down in a domino effect or the son who, with a CIA marksman's accuracy, always manages to say the one thing that upsets you most.

"Mom, you know what I think? I think that as a journalist, you talk about things you don't know anything about."

That's our life. Basically happy all in all, but tired, worried sometimes, and with lots of crumpled clothes.

Not you though! You two seem a perfect couple—ethereal and untouched by the day-to-day accidents that happen in the real world, where the rest of us hobble along taking two steps forward and one step back.

In your previous world, your imperturbable elegance was never lost on account of little things like trying to buy a house and having all the documents in order on the day the deeds are to be exchanged, only to find that one piece of paper lacked the requisite seal. Or finding yourself late for work, stuck in a traffic jam on the day the new boss starts . . .

You two seem able to spend hours together in total silence; reading; discussing politics, theology, or literature; or playing that game you like so much, casting people you know as characters in your favorite novels.

By the way, I took it in good part, dear Agnese, when, just after we graduated from high school, you gave me the part of the idiot in that summer production of Dostoyevsky's play. I remember how you put it: "You are an idiot but in the nicest possible sense of the word." You, on the other hand, were Dostoyevsky's muse. But twenty years have passed since then and I have learned a few ways of the world. I've settled down a bit, just so you know.

It seemed impossible that you two might argue about anything; at most a bit of passion perhaps relating to some noble subject or other, such as the liturgical reform after Vatican II. Ordinary couples, on the other hand, raise their voices about such big issues as how best to load the dishwasher (I actually do load it better). But you were not like us. You were above the common herd and clearly madly in love.

It has to be said that in those days, the biggest issue you had to grapple with was where you would go on any given night—a meal in Rome's Jewish Ghetto perhaps? Or maybe a trip to the theater that you love but Pietro hates. What a hard life you had!

Then your first child arrived and again you managed brilliantly. In political terms, you had a cabinet reshuffle, not a general election!

But now the arrival of baby number two, the second in two years, coupled with you getting that longed-for job (which came just at the worst possible moment while you had two under twos in the home) has brought you down to earth with a bump.

Now you tell me that you and Pietro only sit together if he is giving you a lift to work. Thank goodness you found that lovely Peruvian nanny, though it must be said that she has a very Latin American approach to timekeeping. Her watch seems to offer general suggestions rather than precise information. Could that be a sundial on her wrist?

Now instead of serious analyses of the world political and economic situation, you find yourself exchanging the occasional bit of essential information—we need a quarter pound of ground beef; the appointment for the baby's vaccination is at 9:30; or the insurance renewal is on the shelf.

You are tired, and when silence finally reigns in the house, your first thought is probably not to compose love letters to your man on beautiful, Florentine parchment. You'd rather shower.

Your husband has not had it easy either, his latest gaffe being to forget your wedding anniversary. But you have to forgive him after that time he bought a ticket for the Tom Waits concert he had been so keen to see but then got the day mixed up, so that while Tom was wooing the fans with his distinctive voice, hubby was snoozing on the sofa.

Another thing I have noticed is how annoyed you get at Pietro's lack of coordination, his almost supernatural ability to bump into anything on his path. I can tell your angst by the way you pull back your hair from your forehead, your trademark sign of being stressed, first spotted when we were at school doing a physics exam for which you hadn't studied. You are also stressed out by his irregular approach to helping you in the house, which sees him go from a base level of shameless hiding to peaks of creative enthusiasm when he takes on such pressing tasks as reordering your CD collection according to musical genre, while never seeming to notice that the help you really need is in making the soup.

The launch engine that carried your love into orbit has worn out now, even though it lasted a bit longer than it does for most people. It did what it had to do. It had to pack in, otherwise you two would have ended up in outer space. Now it's time to learn the truth of that old Frank Sinatra song, "The Best Is Yet to Come." You think you have seen the sun, and maybe you have, but you haven't yet seen it shine.

The good bit starts here. Up until now you've just experienced the little sparks of falling in love. The real joy is in transforming those sparks into a sun that warms, that is always there, and that in the end is stronger than death itself.

It's not an easy task. It's a daily, hidden, silent effort that will often be misunderstood, and at the beginning the weight will fall mostly on your shoulders. You are the more delicate and sophisticated half of the couple but also the one who always seems to find the spark needed to get things moving again.

Another word for this work is obedience. Obedience to the promise that you made to the man you chose. But it must be a creative submission: Obedience, yes, but with creativity, always trying to see through the eyes of hope where your love might go, what rough edges need to be knocked off, what defects both of you may need to correct, and what defects you may have to live with, employing a bit of irony as well as a big dose of acceptance.

Hope is important because there will come a time when this second theological virtue seems the only lens through which anything makes sense.

For example, I hope with indomitable optimism that one day my husband might become sociable and talkative, allowing me to invite to dinner even a quarter of the people I would like to have around. How I dream of him welcoming them, like a modern-day Cary Grant, with a cocktail in hand, engaging in witty and intelligent conversation. Alas, a husband like this is but a dream, it seems. Just as it would be a dream to imagine a husband who might wait for me outside the fitting room in a store, offering useful advice such as "Warm colors don't do it for you, darling." Such a man, I suspect, ends up taking you home and then running off with a 23-year-old Moldavian beauty.

Better to hold each other close—even with your defects, when they start to show. I've never met one happy couple who haven't been through this stage. Even you guys had to go through it, which shocked me!

Remember, you are not alone. In fact, you were alone before all this. This struggle is part of the package, the part that's not publicized very much when we buy the wedding package. Maybe there's a clause carried in the small print somewhere or hidden in indecipherable bank-speak: *The indexation rate of the attractiveness of the spouse with whom you contract the agreement above is to be calculated from the gross sum accumulated with the tax deducted quarterly at a rate of 1.02 percent per annum, where year is to be defined as the duration of the calendar year (365 or 366 days).* At the end of the year, if you're not careful, you wonder why the total capital in the relationship bank has gone down.

It's a secret not to be revealed so as not to lose sales. They are all in on it, even the authors of love stories. Have you ever asked yourself why stories end with "and they all lived happily ever after"? What happens just after the handsome prince crosses the threshold with our heroine in his arms? What does he do next? Take off his ermine-trimmed jacket, kick off his boots, and collapse into an armchair?

I like the fairytales that go beyond the day of the wedding, like *Shrek*. I think it's no coincidence that in that film, Mr. and Mrs. are both ogres: that allows them to openly reveal to each other their own baseness, wickedness of character, and repugnant bodily functions. We need to learn this lesson—daily life is not a fairy tale.

The great dramas we all know tell a similar story, from the comic playwright Aristophanes onward for the last couple of thousand years. The outline is pretty similar. It all starts seemingly calm, a new situation arises, a problem emerges (be it obstacle or misunderstanding or loss), and then the final solution. When things begin to spin out of control, the comedy ends. An everyday life filled with passion does not seem to be an option.

And yet it is an option! There's a secret that the world hasn't figured out that allows us to follow a luminous path through the daily grind of boredom, habit, misunderstanding, and annoyances. If I reveal it, maybe it will make me very rich. (If I ever do get very rich, by the way, the first thing I'd do with my cash would be to hire a driver. So that as I travel between work, Mass, athletics, dance classes, catechism classes, and soccer training, I can get time to do my eyebrows, because if I leave them untended for three days, I begin to look worryingly like Brezhnev.)

But back to the secret. It is summed up in one word—sacrifice. The daily struggle is transformed from a stumbling block into another word for love. It's no longer something that gets in the way of love; rather, it's something that nourishes it and helps it to grow. Love doesn't go out in the daily grind; its flame burns stronger.

And please don't tell me that "it takes two to tango"—I expect better from you. You must be tired, or "arrived" as they say in Rome, to say such a thing. Deep down you know that love—which, in Dante's famous words, "exempts no one who is loved from loving in return"—is stimulated by acting selflessly. There's no other way. Keep on giving even while you're running on an empty tank, without ever looking back. Otherwise, what you have is not love, it's a contract, and for that you don't need a husband, you need a housekeeper.

You tell me, with great frankness, that sometimes you have doubts. Let me translate that into plain English for you: You wonder if you did the right thing. Some days you wonder if the whole thing has been a mistake, if you perhaps chose a husband in a moment of weakness. You ask yourself whether you knew him well enough before you got married, and then you think maybe it's you who has changed.

Get rid of these diabolical thoughts! I see the two of you from an outsider's point of view and let me tell you this—he is Mr. Right! No doubt about it. And I'll tell you this too: Doubts such as those you are experiencing are part and parcel of normal married life. I've extorted confessions admitting as much from people who seem to have textbook marriages, couples that you might think deserve a monument to their union, people who in my imaginary museum of relationships would be on a plinth in the main exhibition area with a red cordon around them.

My Aunt Lucia was engaged and then married to my uncle for half a century. (Can you believe that? She only looks about fifty now!) You always saw them together, always content, always united. You might not know that he died not long ago. One day when we were talking about him, I said to my aunt, "Did you ever have any doubts along the way?" Her answer was illuminating. She said, "I'll say only this. When, from the outside, you see the perfect family, always smiling, with all the children sitting up at table, perfect and obedient, mom and dad beaming with pride, that family will have placed a curtain over the window. Such people are cardboard cutouts with background music and canned laughter. Behind the facade, one of them is secretly fuming, saying to himself or herself, 'I'll count to ten and then I'll let them have it.' And somebody else in the family won't even manage to count to ten! But even hidden behind the facade of the 'happy family,' it really is possible for people to love one another very much."

When confronted with the dullness of everyday life, with struggles, annoyances, and burdens that have to be borne, there's no handsome prince (or beautiful princess, obviously!) on this earth who doesn't get transformed into a toad—it's the fairy tale in reverse. You thought it was all about you kissing him and seeing the princely crown and ermine robe appear, as if by magic. But now—at this precise moment—you have to change gear in your relationship. Move up a gear. It's the only way forward.

The only alternative is to turn into one of those people who live in the "what if" world with your head full of memories of those men from your past who seemed crowned with a halo of perfection.

Don't talk to me about that doctor you met when you were doing your PhD in Boston—the one I think exists only in your head! Let's get real—you met for coffee a couple of times. And OK, I know that the giant-size cinnamon-flavored iced Frappuccino at Starbucks takes about an hour to finish, but even so, it doesn't warrant you still pining over him, clinging to his memory like a limpet ten years later.

The other temptation you can fall into is giving way to your fantasies, inventing relationships with people you don't actually know and whom you can mold to suit your preferences. That way you don't have the hassle of having to confront the reality of the person—which is always a bit messy and sometimes a really unpleasant screw-up.

There's the other option—and this is the one men tend to go for—of throwing themselves into work, anything to get out of the house and avoid working on a relationship that's in need of repair—as though any relationship didn't need regular servicing.

We women, on the other hand, tend to escape from our husbands by dedicating ourselves body and soul to the children, and here the risk is more subtle, because no one is ever going to accuse you of being *too* devoted a mother. It may be relatively easy to have custody of the heart, to stop it beating for other men, but children can sometimes take the place of the man in your life even without you realizing it.

And, of course, we can't deny it: there are also times when people have affairs. It's not the sort of thing you can ask people about at high school reunions. But who among us doesn't realize that feelings of boredom and the sense of drudgery caused by picking up one too many dirty socks from the floor can team up with that

person who catches our eye to ambush us? Even the
rather good-looking dermatologist we take the kids
to, with his broad shoulders, his quick wit, and his
way with words can be a danger. Claudia wasn't alert
enough to the danger and look where she is now.

But when you think about it, how do people live
out their affairs—the squalid reality of the clandestine
meetings, the infinite sadness of returning afterward to
find the children at home? How awful must be the fear
of looking into their eyes, worrying that they see that
the reason for their coming into existence (namely, the
love between their mom and dad) no longer exists?

Maybe we kid ourselves that the situation can be
controlled, and it's true that up to a certain point, you
can always turn back. But when you pass a certain
point there's no way back.

My husband, for example, always says that he should
have turned back after our first ever date, when, over
dinner, we discussed the next car I should buy. For me,
only one thing was important—it had to have enough
room for a stroller in the trunk—and we hardly knew
each other!

"I should have known then that I'd soon find myself
surrounded by children," he says. Despite everything
he still thinks he has time to break it all off. Darling,
I have news for you. Time's run out. Over the age of
forty, it would be *so* disloyal—who would ever take me
in a state of near decomposition with four children?

I say all of this, Agnese, just so that you don't
start telling me all about your colleagues at work. I
don't want to know about them. They don't exist. You
can't go around confiding in them every time you have

an argument with Pietro. Don't play innocent with me. Don't be flirting with some American doctor you've found on Facebook as you watch Pietro take the garbage out in his slippers, his pants hanging so low you can see half of his backside falling out the back while his stomach escapes out the front.

There is another option! You could inject a new quality into your relationship. Start working on it again. It's not too late.

In fact, better than that, the first thing you need to work on is yourself. Lately (and please excuse me for saying this), you've been about as much fun to be with as an income tax letter. Maybe it's because you seem to be eating only celery in a valiant attempt to get back into shape—and I assure you, you can after two pregnancies, even if you're out of the running for the Miss Italy contest this year.

You must be tired, I know that, but you are such a perfectionist that you can't bring yourself to ask for help. I think you should try to get the lady who helps you around the house to do a few more hours a week.

There's also the hormone thing, those same hormones that refined your artistic sensitivity, aided your creativity, and bolstered your triathlete's stamina in the business you've been running for years with great professionalism and expertise.

So while you're in the biblical business of taking the beam out of people's eyes, forget Pietro for a moment—the speck can stay in his eye for now. Ask yourself who else would put up with you. Sometimes, you are about as awkward as somebody dancing on crampons. Ask yourself who else would be able to calm you down when you start acting like a Hollywood diva on Sunset Strip who has just discovered a new wrinkle. Ask yourself who else would put up with your strange mental fixations like the one that saw you drag your poor husband around a dozen wallpaper stores to find the exact shade of gasoline green without which your house would have seemed impossibly vulgar.

Let's be honest: Being your husband must sometimes seem like an extreme sport.

So in the face of all those who offer their pearls of wisdom without ever having had the need to balance husband, children, and job, and without having to fit everything into 24-hour days (major problem), in the face of all those who write that love is not so much about looking into each other's eyes but rather about looking in the same direction of travel, I would say, find some way—and fast—to look once more into each other's eyes every now and again.

Organize yourselves. Ask the grandparents to help out. Take a few days off work. Forget about the housework. Take Pietro out. Sit him down and look at him for a while and remind yourself why you married him.

And then, as I have already said, avoid those situations that come very easily to you when you are inclined to be a little bit flirty, especially because you are a beautiful woman and you know it. Even if it won't be long before we are both collectors' items, oddities from a bygone age, you still can make an impact, especially when you've got time to look in the wardrobe and choose what to wear rather than pulling on the first thing that falls out on top of you when you open the door.

Just one more thing (before I start to sound like Good Pope John that night he came to the window of his study and told the parents down below in St. Peter's Square to go home and give their children a hug). I have this advice for you. Don't live parallel lives with your husband. It's a very real danger when you both work together and want to spend time with the kids. Try to keep your common spaces, even when it sometimes feels harder to do something as a couple rather than doing it yourself. Knowing you and your way of doing things, I have no doubt that you would get things done quicker on your own.

I'm not suggesting that you call a family meeting every time you want to move a lamp from one place to another, but some things you really should share. Try to keep doing some activity together as a couple. It's not as easy as you might think.

Remember what Roz the snail says in the film *Monsters, Inc.*—I'm keeping an eye on you (but an affectionate eye)!

Your friend,
C

There's a priest in Perugia to whom a lot of people owe a very great deal. He's called Fr. Ignazio Zaganelli, or to those of us who know him, Doni. He's a man who has the capacity of a newborn baby to distinguish light from shadows. From the pulpit, he delivers judgments that are so blistering that when he turns around, you find yourself looking to see if he has a fiery sword hidden under his chasuble. My views are pretty hard-line, but compared to him, I feel like a progressive politician.

For children like me who went to his catechism classes, it was reassuring to have his solid guidance, free of complicated subtleties. We drank in his words with relief; with him we always knew where the truth lay, and as children it was nice to grasp it quickly and without difficulty.

Then adolescence came along. And with it the idea that we knew it all, the desire to be part of the opposition, and so began the disapproving sighs during his sermons.

But in the end, his parishioners decided that they couldn't do without him and, in fact, through their prayers, brought him back from the edge of death after a heart attack.

I remember once at the wedding of one of my cousins how he completely ignored the groom and spent all forty minutes of his sermon addressing the bride: "It's up to you now, dear bride. The success or failure of the marriage depends on the woman first and foremost. Be a good person and a sweet personality and have an open heart. Be submissive, not in the sense of being dominated or being subject to violence or any kind of pressure, but rather in the sense of having a spirit of service, spontaneous voluntary service to others, ready to anticipate people's needs, and be welcoming."

The longer Doni spoke, the more the smile on the bride's face began to vanish—she seemed to be wondering if she was being set up—while the groom's grin widened, though he seemed to be wondering if he had been forgotten. As for the guests, there was a contest to see who could huff and puff loudest, apart from those like me, who took advantage of the awkward situation to doze off on the uncomfortable wooden pews, despite these having been designed by a sadist. (When you have had a baby awake all night with colic, you can doze off anywhere.) Outside the church, the kindest comment I heard about the priest was, "He is totally crazy."

It's true, Doni is not well known for his mediation skills and considers subtleties a complete bore, but in a way, what he said was right. This is the moment in history when we must throw off the logic of domination, which is a perversion of the man-woman relationship. This was the view of Cardinal Ratzinger, who went on to become Benedict XVI, and the rallying cry of liberal writers like Lidia Ravera and Natalia Aspesi. The point is, though, that you can't dismantle the engine of domination with the tool of emancipation (which in some sense is itself a form of domination or even vendetta). Rather, you escape from these mistaken forms of logic through meekness.

To love one another forever is very difficult—almost impossible, in fact. Those of us who are more generous; welcoming; and able to bring people together, create space for others, and hold things together, we have to be the first to make the effort.

The same Paul of Tarsus who invites us to submissiveness also goes on to say that the day will come when there will be no more man or woman. Meekness is the cure for that domination-based relationship that has marked the interaction between the sexes since the start of time, and that will vanish at the end of time.

I can guess already the names I will be called for having expressed these views: reactionary; fanatic; papist; voice of male religious oppression; a cancerous sexist, poisoning the atmosphere like the cross-shaped antennae of Vatican Radio. These words actually come from a real speech given at a conference, "The Lesbian Subject," which I read later with great interest. The speech called for women to display "a raging and unrighteous anger," which was considered to be the only possible path to liberation.

Call me a reactionary, but I see a great loneliness among women who have stopped making room for others and also among many men who are effectively oppressed by relationships that seem to be more like labor disputes.

I am against a misunderstood sense of equality. I don't want a stay-at-home husband. Everyone should do what he or she knows how to do. The only duty should be the duty to be ready to smile. That smile comes easily to me if a man asks me if I have any nice friends I could introduce to him. Alas, my success rate as a modern-day Cupid is around 1 percent.

If meeting the right person is a kind of miracle, an indissoluble marriage bond must seem the result of one of those incredibly complicated planetary alignments that happen every three centuries or so.

In fact, it's more a question of willpower.

Spontaneity can't be a lifestyle choice or a measure of success or failure. And after a certain point, the emotions no longer have a lot to do with love—or at least they cease to be its dominant feature.

Yet everywhere we look, emotions seem to be just that— dominant. They hold sway in the world of communications, in all the newspapers and news bulletins that scream at us not to use our brains. It's the same at the movie theater. *Dead Poets Society*, a big box office hit from a few years ago, was, when you think about it, an exaltation of emotion for emotion's sake. Emotion, though, is a means, not an end; it's a channel of communication, not content. How can we base everything on this?

The indissolubility of marriage closes off all other side roads for you, but it opens a broad highway for you. You begin to make the effort to love your spouse's defects. You don't go on about them; you in a sense "welcome" them. You stop asking yourself if a particular situation suits you or not. Instead, you figure out how to make it work, since it has to work at all costs.

In this way you begin to live the ordinary events of everyday life (including annoyances, bad attitudes, disputes, and boredom) with love, transforming them. And when you begin to give of yourself, you realize how beautiful this way of living is, and before long, you ask yourself where is the catch. There is none.

Distinguishing between falling in love and loving doesn't mean giving up on your feelings; it's still possible for hearts to flutter after living through countless broken-down washing machines and late mortgage payments together, because sometimes feelings and willpower go together, just like renouncing your own comfort for the sake of others and the experience of pleasure can go together, despite what the dominant culture wants us to believe.

Those couples who thrive, who learn to give of themselves, don't give up on pleasure. It's just that sometimes they need to have a little patience and take the necessary time and make the necessary effort to find that pleasure, peeling it like a sweet fruit consumed amid the complications of everyday life. This wonderful challenge is never experienced by those who live in a world of casual encounters and who imagine their own little love stories untouched by the messiness of everyday life. Theirs seems to be a fabulous way of living: glittering, happy, free, and carefree. But if truth be told, I see none of that in those who have lived through this experience. Rather, those who have trivialized sex find it hasn't done them any good. Where there is no boundary, where nothing is off limits, where there is no experience of the "sacred risk" of conceiving a child, and where there is no sense of achievement (because what we wanted to achieve has been available to us from an early age, at no great effort to ourselves), there's very little left to be proud of.

We women are more responsible for this state of play than men. Thinking we were emancipating ourselves, we've sold out, as we say in Italy, "for a plate of lentils." What we've done is accept the male view of sexuality, hook, line, and sinker. We were the custodians of life, but not anymore. We are emancipated, that's true. We no longer depend on anyone. But in return, we run the very real risk of losing that total reciprocal self-giving between two people that we long for and desire, written, as it is, into our DNA.

The result is that in exchange for our newfound freedom, we are the first to suffer. We are suffering and the whole world is suffering, because if we won't do it, who will guard love for life?

Three Years Later . . .

For many people, marriage is something that goes on in the background while they do other things. Not for Agnese, though. She is married and happy to be married, and the reason is that she understands that marriage is something that needs to be worked at. You have to work—there's no other way—to put the other person's happiness first, even when you realize how difficult it can be. All that's needed is to keep a positive outlook. Agnese, for example, has been known to compare her husband to a kind of wild boar, but having said that she doesn't demand too much from him. She would just like him to be that little bit more civilized—maybe more of a farmyard pig than a wild boar.

The arrival of the children had pretty much transformed Pietro and Agnese from being spouses to being colleagues, working together on a shared task—that task usually being getting to the end of the month still alive! They had become a kind of brother-and-sister act. On top of that, they had to deal with the number one enemy of a happy marriage—routine. So bit by bit, they stopped making the effort to seduce each other, to win each other's heart, to save the best of themselves for each other. (That is, unless you consider it a romantic activity to crawl to the sofa at the end of the day to fall asleep, snoring in unison in front of something on television with the sound turned down low so as not to wake the kids.)

The roommate syndrome is an enormous and very common threat to marriages: Before long, you turn into one of those people who gets made up and dressed up to go *out* of the house rather than *into* the house. That house that is, after all, the place where you should be showing the best of yourself.

Wearing sweatpants and a sweatshirt around the house is, I always think, one of the most obvious signs that the relationship is in danger. I remember I once said this rather incautiously to a journalist who wrote about it in a piece he was doing for a weekly magazine, and from then on every time my own standards slip below an appropriate level, my husband is the first to remind me. "Look at her who goes on about dressing well even around the house," he says when I start to look too much like a dog.

In that same interview, I got a bit carried away and declared somewhat foolishly that when my husband was out working late, I waited for him to get home with a hot dinner ready and the table set for the meal. This description of my efforts made us all laugh at home. I'm sticking to my guns, though. I think I did do that once during our 15 years of marriage. It's just that my fussy family declared that the toasted sandwich that I had prepared didn't count as a hot meal. Anyhow, it would be hard to get proof one way or another because it happened sometime around 2002.

Anyway, my forte is not so much practicing as preaching—so I got three gifts for Agnese to help her in her marriage.

The first was a photocopy of my mom's recipe book. OK, so it might have been more thoughtful to reproduce it in my own handwriting on Fabriano writing paper, but I'll do that when I am one of those retired ladies smelling of Amarige perfume and covered in scarves. My idea was that every now and again, she might want to cook something a little bit special for her husband—even when they don't have guests coming over. Doing that is one way of saying to her husband that he is important and that food is not just a useful commodity to be gulped down as fast as possible.

The second gift was my insistence that she leave her kids at my house for a sleepover on an evening that Pietro wasn't working and the movies that were finalists in the Cannes Film Festival were being shown in Rome. Just a suggestion, of course . . .

The third gift was a nice dress that showed off her figure in a flattering light (a man's reaction is obvious, but it's every bit as important for us women; it reminds us of our own beauty and who it should be directed at).

It seems to me that my friend got the message. Of course, there are still going to be times when, in an emergency, she and her husband will have go into team mode, but these can't be allowed to last too long. The emergency has to end as soon as possible, and normal priorities have to be restored. And among the list of priorities, loving one's spouse is right at the top. We are to love with the same degree of religious observance with which the monk follows his rule of life, taking care of the small details. For us married couples, that might be anything from putting a flower on the table to choosing that nice dress. Sometimes it might seem like the wild boar doesn't notice. But I think he does—and how!

Chapter 7

Elisabetta

Or

We Are on a Mission for God

Dear Elisabetta,

Sometimes, I know, a positive pregnancy test is about as welcome as a kick in the teeth. So much to think about: a boyfriend who sometimes behaves like a 12-year-old, what to do about work and the house, and everything else. I get the picture.

But these circumstances—shall we call them less than optimal?—are nothing compared to the small matter of what's going on inside you. You can give new life. Or rather, you can give your consent to a new life coming into the world. But without your consent, there will be nothing.

There's very small a person who needs you to become that little bit bigger as a person, that little bit stronger so as to be ready to be his or her defender. What do you say? What do you want to do?

142

If you are afraid of losing your own life in some way, you're right; that's exactly what will happen. From now on and for the next few years, you will have to take care of another human being every minute of the day and night. But in exchange, you will get your life back richer, fuller, and happier.

If the problems are purely practical, then don't worry. In Italy, we have a phrase: *Ogni bambino viene col suo cestino*. It means every baby comes with his or her basket. And it's absolutely true. You'll get by. I can tell you that from experience.

Providence is real. God takes care of us, especially when we say yes to life and place our trust in Him without making too many calculations and without counting merely on our own efforts.

In fact the more daring you are, the more generous He will be. I'm not expecting you to do a Mother Teresa act. (I read somewhere that every time she needed a house for the poor, she went to the place she wanted, threw a little medal of Our Lady on the ground, and prayed. And sure enough, a couple of days later, someone would give her the property as a gift.) She was a top-flight saint. But even for ordinary mortals like us, it's amazing how, when we have a baby, things seem to sort themselves out.

You'll pull out all the stops—economic, physical, intellectual, and spiritual—that you didn't even know you possessed. You'll find new courage, daring, imagination, and a superhuman amount of energy. The secret is written deep within us. Children are our future, and even if you don't feel any great maternal instinct at the moment, it will come when your baby is in your arms.

I know what you're like. I know that until a couple of days ago, every time you saw a spoiled brat kid throwing a tantrum, you thought of that advertisement that used to be shown everywhere: "Use a condom." But I am also sure that you will respond to this call of life, since life has apparently chosen to entrust itself to you. I don't know any mother who has regretted having her child, but I do know many who regret not having them. So don't even think of it. The moment that pregnancy test showed up positive, you became a mother. Enough of all these lingering doubts.

You have to defend your child like a tiger, and that means defending yourself from all those who would want to treat your pregnancy as some kind of illness that has to be controlled in every detail.

You're not ill! You might have a bit of nausea at some point, certainly. I remember I was making a documentary in New York when I was pregnant, and my husband memorably asked me, "What do you prefer tonight—would you rather vomit Mexican or Kosher?" And I have to say that New York must be the only city in the world where you can do just that, even on Fifth Avenue, and no one bats an eyelid. The taxi driver stops, waits, and then drives on without a word. "I'm pregnant," I tried to explain, "not drunk!" After all a lady has to hold on to her reputation, even if it's not especially good to start with!

And yes, there will be other annoyances, I accept that, even though some crazy women do succeed in running marathons and climbing mountains with a large bump. I'd say that you don't have to take any particular precautions, except those dictated by common sense. So no bungee jumping from the Empire State Building; don't enroll in any motocross clubs; and don't be like me, whose water burst one time while I was out for a jog. This particular detail (despite the fact that I kept insisting that I wasn't going fast) caused the doctor who had initially admitted me with supreme professionalism to lose his cool (I got a mouthful of abuse in pure Perugia dialect). Of course, it wasn't planned that way; nothing happens in the way you foresee, but there was no harm done.

The fact is that there is nothing that you can predict with any certainty when it comes to giving birth. Faced with such an amazing thing as a new life coming into the world, there's not much you can do other than abandon yourself to the wonder of what's happening, just as you will at the only other event that is comparable: the moment of death.

The only advice I would give is not to oppose the pain. It's not fun trying to "get a roast chicken down a nostril," as the old Italian saying goes, but you get through it just as billions of other women have.

Just don't get too caught up in the advice of the doctors who want to program and check every aspect of your pregnancy and delivery. Often for them it's easiest to resolve everything with an epidural or a caesarean birth (which is very fashionable in Italy right now). Don't get me wrong, sometimes these solutions are a blessed relief, but sometimes I wonder if they are not also real money-makers for the medical team, who leave you feeling that you can't manage on your own.

As for the hypercontrolling tendencies of certain doctors during pregnancy, I have had to flee from several (including a well-known Catholic) who slipped in appointments for amniocentesis tests (which I would have had to pay for, of course) before I realized it and cancelled. One doctor even tried this when I was only 27 and the chances of having a baby with genetic defects (because that's all that shows up) were much lower than the risk of killing the baby in the course of the test. Another doctor once invited me to "hurry up" in having the tests "because Christmas is coming, and if there's a problem with the child, what would we do then?" Basically, she was saying that if the baby was not healthy, it would have to be eliminated.

The practice of amniocentesis is widespread, accepted as the norm, and apparently no longer even discussed as merely an option. The important thing is to know early if the baby has something that's not right, so that the "problem" can be eliminated by killing the baby! A strange approach to therapy and healing, I think . . .

As far as I can see, Down syndrome children seem to be less visible these days, and I don't know whether that's because fewer of them are being born or because more of them are killed before being born. When I saw a little girl with Down syndrome on the beach last year, blond and wearing a pink swimsuit with princesses on it, a bit like my own daughter's, I couldn't help giving a smile of encouragement, recognition, and unbounded admiration to her courageous, affectionate, and heroic mother who could have known before birth and chose not to terminate her daughter.

The poor child of today is forced to play Russian roulette, curled up inside the womb thinking, "I hope they keep me. I hope I pass the test." Even a basic knowledge of science is now enough to realize that what goes on in the womb before birth leaves its mark on a child. That's why so many modern mothers, if their scion passes all the checks with flying colors, make their unborn baby listen to Mozart inside the womb. It would be better if the unborn child could hear a reassuring voice saying, "Don't worry. Whatever happens, we are your parents, and we will deal with it together."

Please remember that if you say yes to life, I will also be here for you as best I can, including providing baby clothes. Because we too—I told you Providence exists—have been on the receiving end of many a donation. So much so that we are now a kind of clearing house for second-hand clothes. Every now and again, someone calls to say, "You wouldn't have a Spider-Man costume for age four, would you?" or "Would you have any boys soccer cleats size 13?"

Yesterday my daughter Livia asked me in a worried tone, "When I grow up and these pajamas don't fit me anymore, what will we do?" I replied, "We will buy you new ones, darling. Don't worry." You wouldn't believe the amazement on her face as she realized that clothes, which normally arrive at our house in plastic bags, can in fact—when necessary—be bought!

So remember, we will be here for you. But more than that, the God of all life will be on your side. And with that assurance, what do you have to fear?

A big, big hug to you and your little baby,
C

Maternity is the first vocation of a woman—not the only one, but the first. It is inscribed in nature and in our own bodies.

During pregnancy a woman is both one and two at the same time. It's quite an extraordinary thing to get your head around and would very probably be beyond a man's comprehension. Not so for a woman, who is made to be two without losing herself, just as she is able to be here and elsewhere, to do one thing and lots of other things at the same time—a capacity utterly absent in a man. From pregnancy on, making room for another being within herself, the woman prepares to make room for others in her house and in her life.

It's a quality found in all woman, not only mothers. Whether it be through having children of her own or not, a woman can always welcome life. It's possible to be maternal even if we choose a different path in life: I know many maternal women who don't have children of their own. They show that quality with friends and colleagues, some even in how they work. There are others who help look after friends' children. For that matter, I have to confess that I know some natural mothers who are not at all maternal.

Those who refuse this vocation to be welcoming toward those who are smaller and needier than themselves—and I include here some biological mothers—tend to end up sad, angry, jealous, disappointed, and resentful. They are divided within themselves. They want to make their mark, but they end up deforming themselves. They have gotten lost, but not through any fault of others, not because of men, power structures, or any other problems relating to the modern communication society. They have gotten lost *on their own*.

Maternity on the other hand offers the possibility of learning that precious lesson of how to give of oneself. And women who learn that lesson move up a gear in life. They flourish. I don't mean to say that all mothers are saints or perfect or even that they are all good. If I even tried to think that, my mind would be filled with a vision of myself—old and abandoned, all my children in therapy, spending years trying to put right my many errors. I can already imagine the oldest one—who has a habit of writing would-be film scripts full of disemboweled spies and horrific explosions—as an old man presenting at Cannes a film about his unbearable mother, a possessive and obsessive figure who looms in the background every time he tries to be happy. We all know the damage that we unbearable, multitentacled parents can do to our children. However, if you try, with honesty and humility, to limit the damage, welcoming a new life into your own life can convert you and help you to be less selfish.

Saying yes to life means saying yes to other things that are not all terribly pleasant, such as having your baby fall asleep—drunk on your milk—with her head lying back in the crook of your arm, completely and irresistibly abandoned to your love, just as you feel the overwhelming urge to scratch your back in a place you cannot reach with babe in arms!

It means saying yes to a car full of fruit juice stains, saying yes to conversations with school teachers who are far more frightening than the director general of state television, and saying yes to afternoons at the movie theater spent on all fours trying to find brightly colored gums, which have a nasty habit of rolling under the seat of the most irritable person on the row. It means saying yes to exhausting and detailed explanations as to why it's not a good idea to hit one of your brothers over the head with a model metal spaceship.

Saying yes to life will also mean feeling an emotional instability at times, feeling the need for reassurance and comfort when your children are in a bad mood and blame you. These same kids who will want to give you big hugs when you are rushing out half an hour late with a tear in your stocking (I often wonder how many times I can use the same excuse in the office: "I just noticed it"). Being open to life will mean cherishing the forlorn hope that you might be able to keep just a tiny section of your desk clear of barbarian invasions, though this is probably only achievable by employing a private security firm with police dogs. It will mean spending the time that others use to enrich their cultural formation or enhance their physical appearance playing with toy soldiers, coloring within the lines, connecting the dots, and more than anything else, worrying yourself silly—about their adenoids, their multiplication tables, their friends, their insoles, their insecurities, and their obscenities.

Despite all that, there is no need to be perfect to make the decision of being open to life, nor is it possible to wait until you reach perfection before trying to bring up decent kids. You just do it as best you can, knowing that none of us are perfectly balanced or free of anxieties. You do it knowing that mistakes will come every day. It's unavoidable but luckily fixable.

We will cook too much meat and too little vegetables; we will defend the teacher tirelessly—even when she is wrong and our child is greatly annoyed; we will expose them to too many ultraviolet rays; we will never quite get the stains out of their T-shirts; we won't buy them the zipper of the right material or supply the nutritionally perfect snack for the school trip. We will give angry looks to the child who makes a mistake, and we will preach the same sermon to them so often that eventually they will recognize the sound and sense of it—without bothering too much about the meaning. (A bit like one of those warnings written on train windows in German, "nicht Hinauslehnen"—"Don't lean out the window." We get the meaning without worrying too much about the words.)

If we commit ourselves with all our strength to limit the damage (a fine ambition in life in my opinion), others will claim we are realizing our hopes and living our lives through our children. This is sometimes said by people who have chosen, for one reason or another, not to have any. It would be good to point out that we were doing OK in self-realization before we had kids, even though we were forced to read, go to the movies, travel, and play sport to fill our time! There are others who will admit, after having discovered late the joy of having a child, that they wish they had known sooner. I know many people like this. They listened to the advice of the world: "Think of yourself first. Realize your ambitions, advance in your career, discover yourself"—as if one could discover oneself alone and not in relation to another person. Then just before it's too late, they have a child, and you hardly recognize them.

I am not a sociologist or a philosopher. I am nothing at all, in fact, but it seems to me that contraception has put in our hands a power that is too big for us to manage—the power to betray our nature and to do so without a worry in the world. No need for courage or honor, just a little sugar and the medicine goes down. We pretend that we are in charge of the game while in reality we give a pharmaceutical company the power to control us—the capacity to control life but also to control our moods, our hair, and every kind of appetite. Everything gets washed away by the illusion that technology and medicine and medication can guarantee us well-being and protect us from unforeseen circumstances.

Even if we leave God out of the argument for a moment, it's clear that no human being can truly control nature. Nature is a bomb that we carry around in our hands and that could go off at any moment in our face. We like to think that we can schedule everything, but how can you plan in advance for something you don't yet know about? This might make sense if we lived in a world where we had nothing to learn, if this life were a journey in which we were tourists looking out of the window taking what we liked and leaving what we didn't.

The truth is we are like dwarfs on stilts; we climb up because we are not big enough even to reach the window, looking in, trying to make some sense of the great mystery that is life. We are poor souls looking for a path to follow. We are dust on the move. Far from programming ourselves, we are utterly impenetrable to ourselves. We are complex beings that no plan could ever explain.

We are a mystery. I can't explain, even to myself, a thousand little details, a thousand little unconfessable follies, dark corners in my being, contradictions that I see in others but to which I am blind with regard to myself. And my blindness to them convinces me they are there!

And all that is before I think of so many other things that I can't explain, such as my selective memory—no power on earth can cause the date of an armistice to lodge there for more than three or four hours maximum, yet the plot of the most hackneyed love story leaves indelible traces. Men's brains, on the other hand, seem to have no problem remembering the important dates of World War I but never those of the next parent-teacher conference at school.

There's so much that we don't understand about ourselves and about life that the only possible response is to welcome it as we find it. We didn't write life's rules, and whether we accept them or not, the rules stay the same. Some are absurd, I agree, such as the fact that that guy managed to become your boss despite the fact he can hardly spell his own name. Or the fact that in Rome there are often two sets of traffic lights at crossroads— one to flash red or green and the other, twenty yards farther on, to catch those who didn't stop at the first set. I don't know why the city council doesn't just employ teams of marksmen to take out all those who stop in front of the white line! It's one of life's great mysteries to me.

Accepting life's rules means adhering to reality. (That means I have to accept that it's neither opportune nor sanctioned by the Gospel to shoot people for not stopping at traffic lights.) Accepting the rules of life therefore means also accepting the truth of things; it means moving beyond your comfort zone and leaving behind your egotism, your hang-ups, and your idiosyncrasies. I am surrounded by people who are unhappy, disappointed, disillusioned, tired, angry, resentful, jealous, envious, and full of made-up needs. We can all feel a bit like that sometimes. Joy, on the other hand, is an experience you begin to know when you stop measuring everything by how it affects you. This opens unimaginable horizons. You begin to live, and in living you begin to understand, because some things are understood not only through your brain but also through your hands and legs and ears.

To go against your own nature, refusing the gift of maternity when it has been offered to you, is first and foremost a betrayal of yourself. That's before we get on to the poor innocent child who evidently doesn't figure largely in your thoughts. What do women gain from this rip-off? I've spent endless hours discussing the issue with my female friends who consider abortion to be a human right. My issue is not with those who make a mistake but rather with those who call the error a "conquest," for words are the vehicles of truth. Alas, I have never been able to get across to them the fundamental issue—namely, that abortion is first and foremost the extreme betrayal of ourselves, and those who oppose it want to protect women from this pain as well as defending the unborn child.

Obviously, my powers of persuasion aren't great. I suffer from a phenomenon I call the *esprit d'escalier*—my best lines come just as I am going down the stairs on my way out. Or maybe my problem is that I get too heated. Or maybe it's just that for someone who has lived through this tragedy of abortion, it is just too painful to admit that she made a mistake, and it's better to shift the discussion.

Mistakes happen. People get things wrong. But that's very different from campaigning for the suffering you have endured to become everyone's right to endure. Why would someone campaign to allow women to do something that will leave a massive burden on their soul and that will be forever very painful to live with.

The only way to lay down that burden is in fact to admit that we got it wrong, and that means calling into question a whole section of our lives. This is a major undertaking, but if you have the courage, it can open up new horizons of freedom.

Probably our great-grandmothers never asked themselves the question whether or not they would be givers of life—with no pill and abortion much more difficult to obtain, finding joy in family life was perhaps the only option. We have to acknowledge that for some, it was a life lived in a cage. So let's not regret the passing of some aspects of the golden era, when people asked for themselves very little, kept their heads down, and struggled on.

Today we can embrace the option of giving life as a free choice, without seeing it as a frustration. For us, it's not an obligation or the only option. Rather, it is a choice that, even if we have studied hard and have the whole world at our feet, is one worth making.

If we accept this option, we leave behind the jaded logic of the world. Every time we allow ourselves to respond to the call of life, we take a real step forward.

When you learn to stay at your post, not only putting up with things, but even trying to love life's burdens, not because you like to suffer—no one likes that—but because you know that your effort is helping another person (it might be your husband, your children, or a friend or stranger), then you are making real progress. My kids would tell you in video game language that you have become a level 42 superhero.

I have seen so many people change in this way and begin to give the gift of life. Not just moms and dads either! Children oblige you in a way to undergo this transformation. It's not only mothers who experience it, but for them the change is immediate and dramatic because from one day to the next, their life is no longer their own.

You no longer decide when to sleep, eat, or take a shower. You no longer decide when you're going to be in a bad mood and when you're going to have a lazy day doing nothing. You no longer decide when to read or make a phone call. Yet I've seen many previously anxious women discover a new inner peace in this loss of control. I'm not talking about poor, frustrated females with empty lives who always felt down but who finally found a purpose in life. I'm talking about doctors, engineers, lawyers, magistrates, and college lecturers—women who have already made a success of their lives and are happy but who at a certain point come to a crossroads and choose the path of self-giving and service to others.

They give up trying to be good at everything, trying to have perfect nails and handbags that match their shoes, smooth skin, and sparkling conversation; they start to care for another person. It's not that they no longer like having matching shoes or a decent manicure, it's just that they like making another person happy even more.

And in return? Dare we ask what they get in return for all this? Well there are all those kisses and cuddles, caresses and moments of holding tight, adoring looks, declarations of love, marriage proposals (from men and women alike!), precious little gifts brought home from kindergarten, concerts at elementary school, and little notes written in a shaky hand declaring, "Mom, I love you" or "Dad is amazing." You also get absolute respect (if mom said it or, even more so, if the supreme authority, dad, said it). You discover you have the gift of healing in an almost supernatural way by means of kisses or hugs, arms that console and chase away monsters, eyes that see in the dark, and words that reveal mysteries.

Three Years Later . . .

Elisabetta had her baby, which almost seemed to arrive as a perfect encouragement for people to have children. Her baby boy has lovely big, dark eyes; has a contagious smile; and is as tranquil as a *bignè* (a kind of Italian doughnut, which the baby resembles also in form, being round in shape and utterly devoid of straight lines). I believe the mom has had no more than three sleepless nights all in. Lucky her—I have memories of months of colic episodes and regurgitations and flu and tepid cloths on the forehead—all multiplied by four and all strictly confined to overnight slots. During those months, I was prone to falling asleep while speaking and making no sense when I did. Some days, I would almost feel tempted to get run over by a car so that I could grab nine, maybe even eleven minutes of sleep on the stretcher on the way to the emergency room.

Elisabetta experienced none of that with her little boy, Francesco. He was a straight suckle-burp-sleep baby, as precise as an accountant in his habits when only a week old. They must have run auditions up in heaven to decide who to send to Elisabetta.

They would have known that her circumstances were not the best, because the baby's dad is a guy who finds it slightly too much of a commitment to buy a season ticket to the soccer stadium ("What if I don't want to go to the match one Sunday?"), despite the fact that he hasn't missed a Roma home match since his father took him to see the great Brazilian star Falcao. He doesn't want to feel trapped. He hates planning ahead, and his reply to every suggestion is, "We'll see." I know that all men have a little bit of that "we'll see" tendency in them, but Francesco's dad takes it to a new level. He hasn't made up his mind to become a father, but he hasn't disappeared out of their lives either. He's there but he's not there. He turns up, but with no commitments.

Despite all this, Elisabetta hasn't regretted, even for a nanosecond, having her baby. Indeed, the very idea that she even considered an abortion now causes her suffering. She can't seem to forgive herself. As for me, I think it's our actions that count. We can't control thoughts that come into our heads. So a mom who thought of aborting her baby but doesn't do it is to me a mom who was a bit afraid, who felt abandoned, or who had fallen under the influence of medical personnel who, at the slightest cause for doubt, told her that her baby might not be perfect and that she may wish not to take the chance and instead "eliminate the problem" right away. I know of literally dozens of cases where a prenatal diagnosis of problems has been made, where the brave mother carries her pregnancy to term, only to find that the diagnosis was wrong.

Having known Elisabetta for a while, I suspected her situation of having a father who was sometimes there and sometimes absent might have devastated her, but no. She maintains a degree of balance and composure that I wouldn't have bet twenty cents on her being able to achieve beforehand. Becoming a mother has totally transformed her. It's made her sweeter, more mature, and more generous, and above all, quite amazingly, it's made her happier. Her only regret may be that she discovered her vocation a little late in life. It's strange. Nowadays, nobody ever seems to say to women that motherhood can make them naturally happy. I try to!

And forgive me, Eli, I'll only say it once and never again because I hate the expression, but just once, very quietly (cover your ears!), I have to say it: I told you so!

CHAPTER 8

STEFANIA

OR

MAY THE FORCE BE WITH YOU

Dear Stefania,

I'm replying to your one-word text message: "Exhausted."

I understand. I know. Having small children around requires superhuman, unutterable effort. But we're not going to dwell on this, right? Those who have never experienced it get bored listening to mothers lighting candles to themselves for their own heroic sanctity. They think that all these stories of daytime and nighttime exertions are a bit exaggerated, while those of us who have been through it and know how tiring all those day and night shifts can be don't need to listen to other people's complaints until our ears bleed.

If you're anything like me, you'll find yourself wondering what on earth you did to fill your life up to that point as a single person living a fulfilling or certainly

159

independent life. A life in which rinsing a couple of plates seemed a bother (though I confess that once, the melon seeds were inside my dishwasher for so long that they began to sprout). Those were days when I could summon up enough brain cells and get them in order and ready for action so that I can tackle a textbook on the history of the Greek language.

Nowadays, it seems hard enough to remember which day the oldest child has to go to school in sweats for gym class, so much so that I have to ask him the same question every week. It's because the couple of neurons left in my brain are running around, trying to deal with too many things at once . . . the new industrial production figures from the government statistical bureau, the money for the cleaning lady, the things the little one has to take into kindergarten, the princess outfit, the various homework tasks, the soccer tournament, and every now and again the need to prepare something for everyone to eat that's not plain, unadorned pasta.

The cry of "I've done it!" will come from the bathroom where your little girl is enthroned at the precise moment you have to drain the pasta, and you'll have two milliseconds to decide between soggy pasta or a dirty bottom.

Be aware that the baby will wake up with Swiss precision just at the moment when you finish loading the dishwasher, or folding laundry, or preparing lunches (do you think the jar of jelly from pre-Napoleonic times can still be used for the school snack?) or when you are gathering together bits and bobs for school projects (where am I going to find a sheet of Bristol red card at quarter after midnight?). Just as you are preparing yourself something to eat to restore some of that energy you've spent during the day and you're opening your mouth for the third forkful, the baby will wake up.

Those activities, which in the past seemed a pain in the neck, like taking out the garbage, now seem like the most relaxing part of the day: "I'll do it, darling!" "No, I'll go, darling. Just you stay where you are."

This task is always better though than cleaning the bathroom, which, with three men in the house, can sometimes seem dangerously akin to fumigating a toilet in a train station restroom.

What advice then can I give you in your baby's first few days of life? Just let it all wash over you. Soon, the adjustments will come; the family will find a new rhythm in which the baby will not be the absolute monarch. Priorities will change, as will your vacation habits (three-year-olds are not that excited by architecture), your friends (three-year-olds and fortysome-things don't always go well together), and your choice of car (at certain points, the baby seat has to go in the front or in the back, and then you'll have to think of places to store the nausea bags, the snacks, and the moisturizing wipes—you have no idea what a mess one chocolate cookie can make).

While you're still in this period of adjustment, walk close to the walls so that if you fall asleep all of a sudden and fall to the ground like a dead body, you won't bump your head too badly.

Kids are at their worst in the evening: sometimes they are irritable, always they are tired, though you would have to hit them over the head to get them to admit that they're the slightest bit sleepy.

By then you will have had to correct homework; feed them (preferably not only with licorice); clean mud stains, regurgitated milk, and/or ketchup, depending on age; prepare school bags and clothes for the next day; and gently accompany them into the land of dreams with bedtime stories, kisses, and prayers, all the while trying to stay calm while delivering a firm no to the most bizarre requests, even though deep down you'd like to buy yourself 15 minutes sleep at any price, even if it meant handing them a whole jar of Nutella to eat under the covers.

It might be useful for you to know that if you need to go to the bathroom and you still manage to retain the right to close the door, you can place a toilet roll against the wall and use it as a makeshift cushion to grab a couple of seconds of rest. Years of experience will also teach you how to adopt a look of deep concentration and almost mystical contemplation at Mass, when you are in fact grabbing a couple of minutes of sleep—on a big feast day, you might almost manage half an hour as long as you avoid snoring. I advise against a snooze at a traffic light—I have done it only to be awakened by the proverbial Roman greeting of an orchestra of car horns and motorists saying, "Look at her. Sorry if we woke you up, honey."

Another useful escape when the situation becomes intolerable and you find yourself promising to solve international emergencies in exchange for a moment's silence is to take a shower. Babies don't stop crying, but once you've convinced yourself that the wail is just a tantrum, you won't hear anything except the sound of running water. To be absolutely sure, it's good to sing at the top of your lungs that old '78 favorite, "Perugia Is a Great Team!" (the Perugia soccer team came historically close to winning the Italian Championship in 1978). You might also try "Staying Alive" by the Bee Gees, which at that point will be more an objective for the day rather than a pop song.

Lowering your expectations is always a wise move, and at certain points, aiming simply to survive is a sign of good sense.

"With your first child, you were always so punctual!" said the kindergarten teacher when I turned up sweating and breathless to drop off a barefooted Livia in the marble hallway because the bell had already rung and I had to rush back for the other three children.

While I was running out, stressing at what might have happened to the others abandoned on the sidewalk, amid the disapproving stares of the other mothers of kids with nonstained clothes and well-combed hair, the phone rang with a note to remind me to buy an end-of-term gift for the teacher. Had I done it? I have a rather strange inability to utter the word *no*, especially when it comes to some task I have been given. Getting the aforementioned gift and running back to the school to drop off the gift with babe in arms—it should be an Olympic sport—in 1 minute 25 seconds is one of my proudest athletic achievements, even though I once achieved a respectable 2 minutes 24 seconds in the 800-meter run.

So lower your expectations, and don't give in to panic if you spot a sock under the bed every now and then or if your legs are not as smooth as silk all the time (give yourself two weeks to get sorted out, but preferably before your husband begins to show too much interest in the woman at the deli counter). If you're not totally up to date with all that's happening in the world, given that you're a journalist like me, just check the headlines every so often to ensure that Italy hasn't declared war or abandoned the Euro currency while you were hand-washing baby clothes with OxiClean. (From the third child on, everything goes into the washing machine.)

It's healthy to reduce your daily expectations and to be more tolerant of your lethargy and imperfections. The kids survive just the same even if the rules of weaning end up getting bent a little. "You mean to tell me that the brown stain around the toothless mouth of your daughter is caused by prunes?" yelled my sister, the queen of health. If you've got the courage, tell my sister—but for goodness sake, don't tell the pediatrician—that the stain was actually caused by melted chocolate. By the time you get to your fourth child, you'd give them a pint of beer and a cigar to keep them quiet long enough to allow you to cook dinner.

It might be better if you were the one to tell my sister a few other home truths, too. Like the fact that when it's midday and all the "good mothers" come in from the beach to protect their kids from the harmful rays of the noon sun and serve them a lunch based on vegetables and fresh fish, I'm often found heading down to the aforementioned beach carrying a couple of baskets of filled rolls—not a vegetable in sight and the closest thing to a vitamin is the orange soda (I imagine it must have had some remote involvement with a real orange at some point).

You will also find that you become much more tolerant of the rules of housework; you too will ask yourself how many green pencil marks there can be on the wall before it needs a new coat of paint. You will relax a bit too with regard to punctuality and with regard to the issue of kids tidying their rooms—if you can still see the bed, the room counts as "tidy." Be confident that all the lectures you've given your kids will one day bear fruit. You may be dead by then, but be sure the fruits will come!

I remember getting a phone call from the catechist accompanying the school trip to compliment me on how tidy Tommaso was in ordering both his room and his backpack.

"Letizia, thanks, but you've got the wrong number. It's Costanza here. Do you not recognize my voice?"

"Yes, I know! You have got such a tidy son. How did you achieve that?"

How did I do it? I certainly don't know. I shouted every night for the last ten years of my life. I picked up discarded underwear, socks, and millions of pieces of LEGOs (we are effectively shareholders in the Danish company). I sharpened the same chewed pencils and recovered school books that had been damaged during the day's shootout in the playground 365 days a year—that's about 4,000 consecutive evenings, all seemingly in vain, convinced that I had the most disordered children of the human race on my hands. (This may be a genetic weakness, given the state of my husband's wardrobe.) And yet? And yet this son of mine, what does he do? He goes on the school trip and proves to be a model student.

So why is he not the same at home? Why is it that at night, when I go into his room, I am tempted to bang my head rhythmically against the wall? I can't even get drunk to forget. I don't drink!

If it helps you to avoid going for therapy when you grow up, dear kids, we'll tell you now why we yelled at you all the time—because you were all complete disasters! Yes, you were marvelous, gifted, lovable, and as sweet as can be—but you were total disasters! You lost jackets, you forgot your homework, you exasperated your teachers, you argued for no reason, and you asked us so many questions that we were left worn out. But we love you!

We love you even when your dad runs up to your room as soon as he returns from a business trip to "Sobby Arabia," and you lift your heads from the pillow just long enough to ask, "What did you bring me?"

We love you even when we take you to an exhibition of Chagall paintings and you seem more interested in a chip on the floor or when we take you to see the magnificent changing of the guard ceremony at the Presidential Palace in Rome and you focus all your attention on the giant cherry-flavor, three-pound giant ice cream cone.

We love you even when you tear each other's hair out to get control of the "wemote contwol" for the "televishin."

Dear Stefania, don't give up hope for the irresistible tangle of foibles that your kids will one day turn out to be. Above all, don't neglect your prayers, which will be more necessary than ever (and very easy to fit into your day when you are breast-feeding—and if you doze off with them at the breast, as my grandma always said, the angels in heaven finish the feed).

Place your children into the hands of their heavenly Father and Mother, and put yourself in Their hands, too. Surrender yourself and your children to Them. Without this thought to guide you, how could you ever reasonably take on this world and all its challenges and help a defenseless little child to do the same?

My second and last piece of advice, before I put you off completely, is this: Learn right from the start to prioritize—a task that I personally find incredibly difficult. My husband correctly defines me as the queen of "fitting in," of the "when you're passing . . . ," of the "while you're doing that . . . ," and of the "if you get a minute . . ."

We women have a tendency to micromanage things, and since the battle is often fought on several fronts, it's easy to lose one's bearings. The trick is to learn a bit of humility and admit that we can't do everything, indeed that we can hardly do anything! So use these days, when your life seems to be turned upside down. These are precious moments in which you can learn to choose, a skill that right now you have to employ. Seize the moment! It's an ideal time to get your priorities right. Learn the new sport that will help you, with great naturalness, to choose not only between good and evil (which is relatively easy) but also between two goods. Which good is more important? Which is more urgent? (The most important thing is not always the most urgent and vice versa.) Which is essential and which is just useful? When you learn this skill, please explain it to me!

You will probably work in concentric circles. The family at the center, and there the Gospel has to be applied to the letter. But be careful. It can seem that the baby is the head of the household when the father should have that role. The idea of spending time with him—the dad—might seem to you to be something you can afford to put off. It won't seem as urgent as changing a dirty diaper. But pay special attention and don't forget to do it. Do it for his sake, for your sake, and for the child's sake because children grow best in a functioning couple. I'm not talking about fireworks, but at least greet each other when you come in every now and again. You can see I know all the theories . . .

I doubt you've managed to read up to this point without dozing off, but if you have, I'm very grateful! There's nothing more enjoyable than giving out advice, even if it's not asked for.

With every affectionate good wish from your preacher friend,
C

Moms of our generation are a bit naïve about the impact of being responsible for another life, one that is wholly dependent on us. For the great majority of us, it's the first time we have completely renounced our own freedom, self-determination, and sometimes our own convenience.

We've grown up with the illusion, and this goes for men too, that we have the world at our feet; every option, every choice, every bit of information seems available to us. Then all of a sudden, when in the course of a day you can no longer choose anything really, life gets a bit more serious. Some men—and some women—can't cope with it.

Personally, I found it pretty traumatizing. I left contact lenses in my eyes (I think there might be one still in there!), I turned up at work on the wrong day, I fell asleep every time I sat down, I walked around in unironed clothes, I lowered my expectations of my offspring (now I merely suggest to them that it's preferable to use a fork to eat rather than to stab a brother in the eye, that it's preferable to put vegetables in one's mouth rather than dropping them elegantly all over the chair, and that it's not terribly nice to tie toy vans to the tail of grandma's cat). I have also progressively reduced the time I spend on my beauty routine, which currently consists of teeth brushing and shower completed in 3 minutes 12 seconds all in. I can only apologize to myself when I read the Ten Commandments of the beauty section in the weekly magazines I persist in buying.

It seems to me that for women, and for men, of previous generations, who drank in the sense of sacrifice with their mothers' milk, the daily struggle was accepted as a fait accompli. They weren't concerned about self-realization, about being "a woman in tune with the times," about their "performance." People didn't ask themselves, "Who do I want to be today?" because the way ahead was pretty much laid out for them. The aim was survival. The list of things to be done wasn't as long as our list, and making room for the needs of another person was altogether simpler.

Please don't consider me an example in any of this. I brought a list of things to do into the maternity hospital because I read that some facilities had a nursery period during the first days of a baby's life, and I figured that I might find myself miraculously with a spare half hour. I thus set myself the goal, as soon as the obstacle that prevented me from seeing my feet was removed, of painting my toenails.

I am hyperactive—like most of my generation—but my husband says that in reality, I am at my most dangerous when I sit down, apparently inert, perhaps struck down by a virus. I gaze into space and, after a little while, proclaim triumphantly, "I have an idea! We could clear those four square yards in the garden, pull out those two trees, and plant another one. We could have a dinner party, a short break, a baby . . ." Nothing is more dangerous than me in a calm moment.

I'm not suggesting that those in the past with lower expectations were always better mothers, but perhaps they were more natural mothers. For them, motherhood was something that was always going to happen in their lives at some point. They didn't feel the need to read manuals or study too much. At some point, life would take over. The aim wasn't self-realization, as it is today—a plan that may or may not include having children. The net result is that the combination of our own selfishness and a society that is profoundly and scientifically hostile to the family means Italy has become the country with the lowest birthrate in the world.

So many moms today are overstressed. The workload is truly monstrous. Work duties, bringing up children, looking after the house, maintaining a film star's appearance, keeping up to date with what's happening—the list is endless. At a certain point, it all becomes one big complaint, as my friend Daniela knows well, being the only person authorized to scold me at regular intervals, a privilege she has taken advantage of often.

I remember calling her, tearfully, the first time the kids got sick: "I'm here on my own! One of them has a fever, one has diarrhea, and the third is throwing up, and I'm here all alone with no one to help me!" Clearly, such episodes only occurred when Dad was out. I mean very out—like Australia or Japan out—and when it was pouring rain and I had to go out to buy children's aspirin and when the grandparents had already been called upon enough.

"I mean, you've got four kids!" Daniela screamed into my ear. "Are you telling me you don't have a crate of kids' aspirin at home? And what do you mean you're alone? Who do you expect to look after your kids other than you?"

After a few of these exchanges and a variety of emergencies, I too realized that I had to roll up my sleeves and stop looking for other people to come to my aid. Sure, it has happened that I've had to go to my neighbor to hand over a wet-diapered newborn because I had to deal with three other simultaneous emergencies. I've also had to call on another neighbor—a man this time—because a lizard had taken up residence in my bedroom. But that's another story . . .

My point is this: It seems as though we have forgotten how to be natural mothers to our children. I can't explain why. Maybe the wisdom of generations past is no longer being passed down. Maybe we don't have enough grandmas and aunts in the family home. They have been replaced by advice manuals, experts, speech therapists, educational psychologists, and doctors whom we consult at the slightest whim.

Now we have play centers (!)—places where we take them to play for a fixed fee and a fixed time, as though play for children was some special activity and not simply discovering the world around them. We now suffer from the curse of "party animators," who force kids to take part in hideous sing-alongs rather than just leaving them to run about freely, to make lots of noise, even to squabble, without adults sticking their noses in. If kids are no longer free to play in squares, streets, or courtyards, where will they learn to survive and make it on their own, even if that does involve the odd fight and the odd punch being thrown as they prepare themselves for what awaits them in the big bad world?

And let's not even mention the cruelty of those Christmas villages with their baby parking facilities, where children—according to their enthusiastically selfish parents—can be handed over and forgotten about for a few hours. Day care centers? I don't want to forget about my children, if you don't mind! Especially not during the holiday season—vacations should be the family time par excellence. Vacations should be a time when we give our children our time, when we listen to them, when we rediscover the beauty of taking it easy, when we have a right even to get bored—which is actually a very useful opportunity for them to get to know themselves better, to discover new depths of creativity, and to open that book that mom has been trying to get them to read for the last year.

At the other extreme from the baby parkers, you find the professional parents—the ones who have heart failure if they suspect their little pride and joy has sampled a drop of Coca-Cola or if the baby food isn't organic, the medicine nonhomeopathic, or the cotton that comes into contact with little darling's skin nonorganic. Only if all these precautions have been duly observed will the kids be able to start their musical studies at the age of three and at six their CV will be embellished with foreign language study, fencing proficiency, and rugby training. So much effort must be expended to achieve the perfect child, one who will at least be a candidate for a Nobel prize, an Olympic medal, or an Oscar—it's just a pity that the poor kids are never taught why they were brought into the world or where they're going.

The truth is that being a parent is about loving, being welcoming, and giving your children permission to be themselves. It's also about helping them find the right path, remembering always that it's not us alone but God too who is helping them grow and willing them on to real success. This knowledge protects us from useless anxieties, stops us giving way to fear, helps us start again as often as we need to, and helps us not feel shattered when all our efforts seem to be in vain.

Three Years Later . . .

If one more person says to me that Italian proverb "Little kids, little problems. Big kids, big problems!" I will scream. It may be the case that both Stefania and I are past the stage of diapers and breastfeeding, but from where we're standing, there ain't much light visible at the end of the tunnel, so if problems are only likely to increase as the kids get older, I might just take to the bottle!

A working supermom is constantly about six days behind in her schedule. Only if the rest of the world (including her offspring) went into hibernation for a week and she was able to work day and night would she have any hope of getting back on an even keel and tidying her house to an acceptable standard. (And even then, mass hibernation would have to exclude vital occupations such as postal workers, vaccination clinicians, school secretaries, accountants, hairdressers, cardiologists, pediatricians, and all the other groups she has to catch up with.)

It's nigh impossible to hurry through other tasks if every time you are free from work, you spend all your time picking up things that one of your four little darlings has discarded during the day. I have a daughter who could graduate in a new discipline—philosophy of laziness—and I sometimes think that my house has been transformed into a world-leading center for this study. Actually to say my kids are lazy is not quite right. Let's just say that they always have something better to do when you need them to be useful around the house, do their homework, or anything else that does not involve throwing themselves out of lemon trees, reading trashy comics, or lying on their bed dressed as princesses on the off chance that some friend of their brother might pass and kiss the sleeping beauty. They are also very good at hiding themselves in secret dens protected by hand-written signs declaring, "No Entry to Philistines or CIA Agents."

Don't think I haven't read all the manuals about how to get their attention and get them to live orderly lives, and I do try every so often, but if you are like me and have all the charisma of a toaster, there's not much you can do. Anyway, I'm not the only one they don't have time for, as this recent exchange revealed:

"Mom, why does Fwanca say the wosawy while she teaches us to embwoider?"

"Well, darlin' Jesus did say we should pray at all times."

"Well, I'm sowwy, really sowwy, but you'll have to tell him that I just can't. I've got too many other things to do."

Despite the constant struggle, we live in the knowledge that there is not going to be any letup. (Neither my friend nor I belong to that special category of families who have grandmas desperate to take the kids away for a month in the summer for a beach vacation. Even two days would be nice, but unlikely!)

"Bernardo, get up and pick up the LEGO. Why are you so lazy? How can you still be tired?"

"Mom, I've taken eight bullets in my stomach and all the rest is whisky."

"Oh well then, you must be tired after all . . ."

Despite the disappointing lack of success, despite the horse-dose pills of hope that we have to consume regularly, a mom is called to see her kids for what they can one day be, not what they are at the moment. We have to see their potential. This capacity is almost miraculous—it's a bit like when Peter walks on the water, he manages just fine until he looks down and sees his feet on the waves (see Mt 14). It's the same for us. The hope-filled gaze fixed on the future is essential for parents, especially for mothers who sometimes feel they are suffocating in their own anxiety over their kids' imperfections.

The writer, academic, and educator Franco Nembrini explains it well. He once asked his students to analyze the phrase "My mom loves me." One boy wrote the following: "My Mom is a use of the *possessive*, no, *obsessive* pronoun followed by a noun." The prof gave him ten out of ten for this penetrating grammatical analysis.

If we try to see our children differently—loving them tenderly but not seeing them either as our possession (love is the complete opposite of possession) or as a projection of ourselves, and certainly not as the result of all our efforts, our children will end up converting us.

Besides flushing out our selfishness, they teach us to see ourselves differently. We see people who are doing their best and playing their part but who recognize daily, in their own weaknesses, the strength and support of their true Father in heaven.

"You're not my real mom," said one of my daughters to me one day. It wasn't that she was angry with me. Indeed, the opposite was true. It was said in a tender moment. "You are my sister. My mom is Our Lady."

What peace I felt sweep over me at those words. Finally, I could relax.

But then I began to wonder . . . will Our Lady know where to find the vaccination record book?

CHAPTER 9

ANTONIO

OR

YES YOU CAN

Dear Antonio,

As far as I can tell, the biggest difference between a father and a mother is that the former seems to have an absolute inability to recognize bugs and adult lice.

Guido, despite being a splendid father to the same four children to whom I am the mother (what a coincidence, that!), is totally ignorant of what these lovely little beasts look like, which filled me with such delight as I engaged with them most nights last winter!

My kids, through coming into contact with a total of about 100 friends, have put our family at the forefront of a major parasite emergency, several waves of it, and cost us an arm and a leg in remedies (so much so that my local pharmacy has a picture of me up on the wall under the heading "Our Benefactor").

For this reason, head lice have been at the forefront of my nightmares for the last year with far greater frequency than those previous demons I had to deal with—the athletics coach telling me that I had wrongly signed up for the Olympic 10,000-meter final or the teacher of linguistics telling me that my homework was all wrong.

I fought for months with the unwelcome little guests, which, you should know, are very resistant to high temperatures but die easily if put in a freezer. This information would have been very useful for me to know if I only had a freezer big enough to store four full sets of kids' clothes, jackets and hats included, and four sets of sheets and pillow cases, as well as quilt covers.

I fought on alone for months, struggling with my bare hands, meeting my husband on the stairs on the way out, asking him hopefully and innocently, "Did you check?"

"No problem. Don't worry. There was nothing."

That night, in a "just to be sure" moment of scrupulosity, just before putting them all to bed, I took the comb and passed it through their hair only to find a line of nits long enough to dance a jig.

In the two or three hours following, I apply treatment number one, an operation that drags on past midnight. By now the little ones, shattered by their lack of sleep, are in tears because apparently they can't get to sleep without that two-inch-high princess doll—the very one that we can't find. Meanwhile, the big one remembers that he must, at all costs, find a set of compasses for the next day's test (which, funnily enough, is not one of the items on the menu at the local pizzeria).

Amid the general hysteria, Bernardo, who is also worn out and sleepy, lets out one of his legendary moans, this time because he's just remembered that he didn't get the Roma soccer top that he wanted for his birthday, the one with the name Menez on the back (Menez, from what I can understand, would appear to be a soccer star). Well of course he didn't, because all the boys want the traditional dark-red Roma shirt with the name of the legendary strike Francesco Totti on the back, but not our Bernardo. Our little lateral thinker only wants the one that you can't find in the shops.

I sometimes think that when you look at me, dear Antonio, and see how kids have turned my life upside down, it doesn't exactly encourage you to have children of your own. But remember, you will be a father, not a mother, so don't compare yourself to me.

First, because I—as you well know—am exaggerated in everything I do. If I read the spiritual classics of the desert fathers, I want to become a hermit. If I find an author I like, I feel the need to stay up all night every night until I have read every word he has written. So when it comes to motherhood, I approach it in the same way—seriously! Maybe sooner or later, I will realize that there are no medals to be won at this task and that most importantly it's not us but someone far greater than ourselves who makes the children grow.

Then there's the fact that I am a female and I therefore can spot the larvae in a child's head. You being a man will be exempted from this task. Not because the head lice would ignore you (though on your head, they would only be able to skate!) but simply because you are male.

You'll have loads of other duties to fulfill, but you'll manage them all marvelously.

Besides which, you won't have to breastfeed and you won't have to know either the location (in the medicine cabinet, funnily enough) or the dosage of the tablets for reducing the kids' temperature. You won't have to know the names of all the teachers (unless they are particularly good-looking, I presume) nor their taste in flowers. You won't have to store in your head the names and birthdays of literally dozens of little friends. You won't end up going to their parties and therefore won't end up getting involved in discussions about the last school trip that, anyway, you would barely be aware of. You won't know the dates for the next vaccination; the next visit to the orthopedist or ear, nose, and throat specialist; or the next eye test. You won't have to brush up on your knowledge of Piedmont or of subtractions sums involving carrying amounts forward. You won't be expected to talk at length on the color that goes best with each little princess. You won't have to tell the story of "Adam and Diva" until you're hoarse and you won't be asked to sing "Be Not Afraid" in the middle of the night after a child's nightmare.

On the other hand, you will be for your child kind of like God—the only person on planet earth who can solve their problems, make things, change batteries, find solutions, give definitive answers, kill monsters, and banish fears. You will dictate the party line, and when Chiara, who is as soft as me, feels as though she is about to be overwhelmed, you will be the one with the clear-sightedness to recall the great educational principle of Jean Kerr—"We're bigger than they are, and it's our house." Even if it doesn't exactly follow the insights of the great Dr. Spock, that line does manage to achieve peace in the home.

You will have the gift—one shared by all the male sex—of selective hearing, which means you won't have to answer every time someone asks you to do something.

You will be programmed with a highly tuned sensor that will allow you—unlike mothers—to know when it is really necessary to get up in the middle of the night when the kids cry to see what's wrong.

You will have that gift of being able to answer, "Oh really?" with an almost English sophistication to every piece of news that comes your way; especially if you're busy watching the Milan soccer match and the news you're being given relates to the lost toy rabbit. You'll be able to emit a convincing "wow" every time you hear about an exciting bowling game at which your son won 27 new toy figures.

You will be able to watch your offspring with the same level of interest as you look at the minutes of the community council meeting without your cover being blown because they adore you anyway, even when your thoughts are with the missing adjective in the article you wrote two hours ago rather than with them.

As a male, and therefore capable of compartmentalizing your thoughts, you'll know how to switch off. You'll be able to say on the phone, "I'm just about to do the biggest interview of my life, I've got to go."

A mom, on the other hand, being female, manages the confusion—even with a minute to go before doing a live television report, she will answer her cell phone fearing the potential disasters at home: Someone might have swallowed bleach or got super glue in his or her eyes.

As a man you will be able to resist the worrying but well-planned nighttime laments: "I'm not feeling well."

Such traps are set by the astute child who would do anything rather than sleep, even go and visit Aunt Sandrina.

"Anyone who's not asleep won't be able to come on the day out tomorrow."

"But I'm scared."

"Scared of what?"

"Scared of that yellow monster up there."

"It's just the reflection of the light on the curtain."

This is the reaction of the lucid, calm father, if he ever makes it to the bedroom!

For a mother, it's oh so different. She's immediately plunged into panic. "I've got a fearful child, so I must have made a mistake in their upbringing. It's all my fault. I must reassure him, but what do I do in this case—stick to the rules or make an exception? Try to minimize things or console him? Raise my voice or give him a hug?"

Thus progresses a whole psychological drama that takes place in the silence of her head and all in the time it takes for the father to go back into the kitchen, pour himself a glass of orange juice, scratch himself, and lie down on the sofa.

Fortunately for you, the kids won't take offense or stop talking to you, as I do when your distractedness interferes when you are supposed to be talking to me. Or as happens when your efforts to squeeze in too many appointments in your day mean that you skip that coffee we were due to meet for once too often, just when I need somebody to shout at!

For children it's not the same. They stick like glue. You can give them the sternest of reprimands or even say something horrible and unfair to them in an effort to grab 13 minutes to shut your eyes and put your head down somewhere—anywhere—to sleep. A minute later they'll be back inviting you to do a puzzle with them because they have forgiven you. They are the magnanimous ones giving you the chance to hear their list of best friends listed by points or, if you prefer—this is really good for a laugh—according to shape of head!

You will somehow know whether to respond in a red, yellow, or green way, rather like a traffic light, in deciding which child to pay attention to first when you get home from work and are immediately overcome.

You'll also know when is the right moment to give them a slap, sure of your judgment and free of those maternal doubts that assail us moms: Could a smack make them insecure? All the while you know that if they merit a smack and you don't give it to them, it's you who will be insecure.

As a father you will know how to choose. You'll know when is the right moment to put your book down. (Usually, it's when you hear a voice say something along the lines of "I think that's a piece of lampshade on the floor." At such times it's usually best to check out what's happening in the soccer match taking place in the living room!)

For all these reasons, I have decided. You and Chiara must make babies! My decision does not allow any grounds for appeal. You are too well matched to not know what would happen if you went for it. And even if I don't know Chiara all that well yet (I trust your choice though), I know you! You are my best friend of the other race—the male race. You are too talented, too intelligent, too sensitive, and too special to allow all your gifts to go to waste.

You are also gifted with the best sense of humor I've ever come across in another human being. Maybe if I ever meet the comic actor Walter Fontana, I might have to review my judgment, but for now you're number one. You make me laugh even when you whisper a monosyllable to put an end to my ranting in which I may have said the worst things ever to have emerged from a woman's mouth. On that occasion, you prudently realized that it was best not to contradict me, and with one four-letter word, you managed to make me laugh until my sides were sore. "Ecco," you said. ("There you are.") Not one word more was needed.

The more I think of it, the more sure I am that you will love all the new material for humor that your kids will supply you—for example, when they enjoy the film clips you show them or read the books you suggest for them.

A couple of days ago in my house, I couldn't help laughing as Bernie defended himself against an attack from his brother by brandishing a smelly item of wool, shouting, "I've got a sock here and I'm not afraid to use it!"

Or on another occasion when I lift them out of the bath and he puts on blue sunglasses and announces, "My family has caused me grave psychological problems. I hate the world. I hate everyone." That was Bernie, too, the joker.

You will also enjoy the theological discussions that take place in the bathtub, when from the kitchen, you will hear them debate, "Did you understand what Mom said about what happens after you die? I mean, do you go up into heaven or down under the earth? And what happens to horses?" You can't allow all your gifts to go to waste; you're too much of a genius to just be a journalist.

Maybe you could just start with one child at a time. At the beginning there will be two of you against one, and you'll do just fine. I can see you already, crawling around the baby's feet, totally unconcerned about your image, dressed as a Native American, a pirate, or even a handsome prince. Because if you have a little girl, I think you'll be more than happy to play the handsome prince. I have the address of a shop where you can buy a two-tone princely leotard at a rock-bottom price if you ever need it.

The only doubt I have at all would be about how much support you might be to Chiara. Personally, I wouldn't even ask you to boil an egg. I can't imagine you changing a diaper, but you might say these are mothers' jobs. But the trouble is I can't see you doing too many dads' jobs either, like stopping the car to load the stroller into the trunk with a line of cars honking their horns behind you while the baby throws up all over your suit, the one you chose for that live broadcast from the courthouse. That scenario is likely to play out on the day the director has called you to say that they need a live report for the early news two hours earlier than you had expected.

I laugh at the very thought of you, who normally struggles over your appearance (do you still polish your lenses with slices of bacon fat and did you ever find those keys?), becoming responsible for another human being. But these things don't really matter. Let the car horns honk while you kick the stroller for the umpteenth time or gaze at the word *tirare* on the frame. (Does that mean push or pull? There's no way of knowing—you only slept four hours last night.) As for your suit, who is to say that the regurgitated milk on the shoulder look might not become fashionable? The bottom line is that even you will learn, although you are starting from a low base line, just like we've all had to learn. Tell the truth, would you have given a dime for my chances when we met at journalism school?

The main thing is that you are one, big, solid, trustworthy, walking distributor of affection; a great listener; and capable of intelligent understanding and love. All you've got to do now is narrow down the number of beneficiaries of your gifts. Your core business will stay the same—all you need is a new business model.

All of us who form part of your enormous circle of friends (how do you remember everyone's name?) will be happy to line up in an orderly fashion when your baby arrives to take the place of honor.

You will know how to be a wonderful initiator of life, attentive, ever present, and full of goodwill. The baby born to you and Chiara will be lucky; indeed, you will share with him or her a tremendous cultural formation, a love for your country, and an original worldview. If it's a boy, you will be his model; if it's a girl, you will become an official provider of love, and she in turn will love as she learned to love from you.

As for Chiara, I don't really have the right to give her advice. We don't know each other well, yet. She will have her own friends, but I can't wait to see her when she comes to Rome. It's a given that she is as unique, special, and precious as you say and very, very smart. She has also accepted the crown of martyrdom in being with a man who is quite unsuited for the complex difficulties of life, such as wearing clothes that match, meeting the deadlines of his long-suffering accountant, and remembering which key goes in which lock when he comes home from work each day.

I'm sure she will be too intelligent to make the mistake most new moms these days make—the one that I certainly made. She won't hand the kids over to you as soon as you come in from work as though she should be compensated for having been at home with them all day and as though you had done nothing up until that point.

If you speak to my husband Guido, he'll be able to give you a bundle of examples of that kind of thing— times when I couldn't wait for him to get home from work so I could go and lie down for a nap instead of trying to provide him with some form of semidecent meal and a welcoming atmosphere. The kind of atmosphere that might make him want to be there at home with us rather than at the dentist to get a filling or at the tax office to go over his annual return—anywhere really to get away from my moans and escape from the requirement to take orders from a petulant wife who finally has in her clutches someone to listen to her and who is more than three years old.

It took me a while to realize that a husband is not a babysitter and that he therefore has his own way of dealing with the children and that mothers can't control everything and influence every detail. Certainly, she shouldn't do this in front of the children, who should never see the division caused by the mother challenging the father. It's not good for them. If there's something to be said between the parents, let it be said elsewhere, not in front of the kids.

I also think there are certain standards to be maintained even when you are totally comfortable in each other's company; standards that mean mom should not be opening the door for dad at seven o'clock at night dressed in a gown and slippers. In my case, I went further and discouraged my husband from being present at the births of my children—I had the feeling that I wouldn't be at my best at that time and that I would have struggled later in the role of seductress! But this is a personal choice that I would not presume to give advice on.

Not sharing absolutely everything (and by that I mean the least attractive elements of our personality) is, I believe, a good rule to follow. Not all anxieties need to be voiced openly as soon as they arise (I have a habit of diagnosing devastating fatal illnesses among my family members repeatedly during the day). Not every bad mood has to be revealed openly. Not every limit of good behavior needs to be thrown off because we are put to the test by the upheaval of a new lifestyle.

What is it that they say? If you ignore crises, the crises will ignore you.

And besides, the new life that you will live won't be as overwhelming as you fear. It has already been experienced billions and billions and billions of times. Normally, people survive. If necessary they change gear.

With all my love and a big hug,
C

Once upon a time, fathers were absent figures—and not only those who came back from the war to find children conceived years before whom they had never met. (In the diary of a family friend born in 1942, one entry read, "Dad in Greece. Gino born." He wasn't trying to be funny. It was true!)

Back then, even when the dads came home, it was as though they were still away fighting, though now their absence was due to work, which was often far away; tiredness; or sometimes just distraction.

If one of their wives had asked them to change a diaper, they would have looked at her with incredulity, as though she had asked him to go out into the garden to wash a giraffe!

When he was around, the father was often a pest who gave the rest of the family a hard time—at least so it seems from the stories I've heard over the years from previous generations. But "giving them a hard time" also meant being a figure of authority, one who set the rules and who imposed the standards of behavior expected, sometimes using very convincing arguments, arguments that in those days include a disciplinary slap when necessary.

To write a short history of fatherhood would be a hard task, but I think it's fair to say that at a certain point halfway through the twentieth century, it was decided somewhere that "authority" should henceforth be counted as a swear word.

Of course, it's quite true that bringing up kids in an atmosphere of terror, getting them to behave by threatening them with a firing squad, is not the ideal educational approach. But if I had to choose between that approach (which didn't always produce such great results) and the current method of democratically consulting the child over every issue that may impinge on him, I can see certain advantages in the former!

In reality, the main problem with that old-fashioned system of child rearing was that authority was sometimes stupidly applied. It wasn't so much a question of harshness as stupidity. The father would impose his authority without caring too much about who he was dealing with simply because it was his right to do so. He did not always act with intelligence, generosity, or dedication, and too rarely knew how to listen.

Now, children are listened to. We bend over backward to understand them, but we don't seem to have the courage to teach them to respect firm and fair authority. It's as though we are afraid that by doing so, we will hurt or disturb them. We don't realize that the greatest gift we can give our kids is to show them love, that love that is a secure and safe path through life but not always an easy one to follow.

Essentially, I think the lack of authority, and sometimes of authoritativeness, comes from not setting our sights high in life. The word *Auctoritas* in Latin is related to the words *augment* and *accrue*. But augment and accrue in what? Which direction? Up or down? We haven't a clue. We could use one of those boxes that wineglasses come in with the arrow showing which way is up in our lives. (I know all about those boxes, having not paid attention and smashed a dozen new glasses that were given to me as wedding presents. Auntie, if you are reading this, I'm so sorry! If you did feel like buying me replacements, though, it was the one in pink crystal.)

We live in cities without cathedrals. We rarely, if ever, lift our gaze. How can we ever convince our children that someone up there is watching over us if we never lift our heads, if we're not convinced of that fact ourselves?

In the past you didn't need a particularly strong personal religious conviction. All you needed was to live in a Christian culture of shared values, learned patterns of behavior, and ultimately common sense. You didn't need to buy a book to figure out how to do everything—how to potty train babies without tears; how to get kids to go to bed without tantrums; how to get them to eat without watching television. There was always an aunt around who had been through it all a half-dozen times without any great hassle, and all you needed from her were some basic tips. You would have seen all these things happen in your large, united family.

But for those of us who became parents after the revolution of the 1960s, the instruction manual was whipped away from under our noses. Panic set in. Is this how we do it? Will this cause the little one a trauma? Will it disturb him? So we make it up as we go along, with rules and roles in continual and exhausting evolution. Nothing seems natural any more. There are some old-school parents, the make-them-read-Tacitus-in-Latin approach, and others of more liberal tastes who have their 12-year-old spoiled rotten—theirs is more of a let-them-read-Tacitus-in-bed approach. Then there are some parents who put TVs and computers in the kids bedrooms to do with as they will. No Tacitus at all for those kids!

Most of all there are armies of parents worn out by the shattering, all-encompassing experience of child rearing and perhaps for that reason not too keen to repeat it too often. They are left lonely and disorientated.

The park is a good place to observe this phenomenon. You begin to chat, and the conversation soon gets around to children—what a surprise—and you come across mothers, especially those who are a bit older, who are jaded by the whole experience, tangled up in their own doubts. Or you might come across another type—even worse—who exalt their own efficiency in having their poor child take part, from morning until night, in an endless array of activities that they rattle off with pride. For the record, I should add that there is also a minority of normal women with whom one can even chat about politics or movies . . . because for me, anyway, when I go to the park, I don't want to talk about breastfeeding or biological baby food. I've had enough of it!

As for the fathers you meet on such outings, I would like to bring in a new law that would forbid them from bringing babies of less than 12 months to the park. We need to protect men from the dangers of a feeding bottle that might be too hot or too cold, of changing diapers on a park bench, and of a dropped pacifier that falls on the sucking end (it must be a law of physics), ending up beautifully smeared in gravel that the dad will have to lovingly suck clean.

If men and women are different and not even distantly related, and if for a man, taking care of a baby is an enterprise requiring superhuman effort—while for us it's not easy, certainly, but it is a pleasure—why would we oblige him to do it for the sake of some equality or sameness that doesn't exist and never can?

Why do men not have breasts? And don't say because they would always be touching them! Why do they not give birth? And don't say because if they could, humanity would become extinct because it would be too sore for them!

The family is a team in which every player has his or her role to play, the one that comes most naturally. The secret of living in harmony is recognizing the talents of each person and giving him or her the opportunity of using them. Sometimes this requires a little smart thinking:

"Darling, do you think you could maybe find something on the Italian lakes for the high school project?" can be a good way of leaving a tired man alone in front of his beloved computer. For his part, my husband sends me out for a run when he hears me clattering about angrily, putting the pots and pans away with just a little bit too much vigor. When I come back, I have usually forgotten why I was angry in the first place.

So when I see dads fumbling about trying to look after newborn babies, I ask myself if they are truly content in that effort or if they are doing it because their wife is making some point about a misunderstood question of equality. Equality is about having equal dignity as human beings, not about doing exactly the same things. Let each person do what he or she is best at!

In man's DNA is written the *nomos*, or the law, the rule. This equates to the role of the father. It's an important role and a tiring one because it's almost always easier to say yes than no to kids' requests. The father, though, indicates the right path and helps to choose.

The father proposes values and objectives and does so always respecting the child's freedom. This is what Don Giussani, the Italian priest who founded the Communion and Liberation Movement, defined as the *rischio educativo*—the educational risk. It's a risk that often a mother doesn't have the courage to take, being more inclined to worry and be afraid of something going wrong.

The good father, sure of his ideals, also has the courage at the right moment to sit on the sidelines from where he can watch his son go out into the world, sure that he has given him clear coordinates for the future.

Values have to be nurtured. Young people need to be shown trust and esteem through a good example, through understanding and a listening ear, and through a loving atmosphere in the family home. And this is something that the parents are called to do together. When the time comes for the son to leave, it's the father who gives him the courage. He has done it himself; he has lived the rule in his own life.

Sometimes the father also has to know how to be merciful, as with the prodigal son. But what mercy can there be without laws? What transgression are you forgiving if there was no rule in the first place?

The educational crisis of today is largely down to fathers who no longer act as fathers and to mothers who don't help them to fulfill that role. You can't expect a dad to be both a babysitter and also a figure of authority.

I asked my kids what was the difference between mom and dad.

"Mom gets angry, and then she thinks about it, and then she forgets it. With Dad, it's different. If he says something, that's it."

I'd say that pretty much sums it up. Except, dear children, I don't *only* get angry. Right now, I can't exactly remember when, but there must have been some times in the past when I was nice!

And please don't call me Little Miss Crashbangwallop. And while I'm at it, it's not true that I am like an East German Olympic judge. (What would they know about such things? They were all born at a time when the Berlin Wall was being sold in fragments to tourists in a reunited Germany) One thing you say about me is true, though: I do forget everything. Deep down, there's method in my madness!

We women struggle more than men with rules. From the time of Eve on, planted deep within us, next to the seed of welcoming, is the seed of rebellion against laws. Ask us to do anything; anything at all. As my daughter Livia once said to me, "Tommaso has gone out. Now Mom can take over."

You can strip us of everything we've got, but please don't ask us to be fathers. That's one role we can't play.

Three Years Later . . .

Antonio still hasn't decided to become a father, and this is one major waste for humanity and for me personally. It would have been priceless comedy for me to see him getting to grips with those practical tasks we parents have to perform every day while he keeps on reading (I do admit it) intelligent articles.

I had prepared a list of the most awkward baby clothes for him—like those baby suits that come as a single garment with spaces for the feet at the end of the pants (don't tell me that you haven't had the experience of trussing up the poor baby trying to get two little feet down one leg). Or the dreaded baby jacket that comes complete with a federal judge and a stopwatch to time how long it takes you to get the ribbon through the right buttonhole (anything above six minutes and they take away from you your kingdom and all your powers).

Probably Chiara would never have asked him to go to such lengths, but I would have given them the items as gifts anyway, hoping to see him, as the years rolled on, coming to terms with the challenges of parenthood: explaining the financial markets' spread to a wide-awake six-year-old—to do that you'd first have to understand what it is yourself!—or carry on a conversation with a daughter who confided to you her greatest secret the day before, a secret you can now no longer remember. (Antonio, here's a tip for you: Always press "Save" before you turn off your brain.)

But it wasn't to be. Antonio and Chiara split up. And this teaches us—well it teaches me; you already knew—that in the end, our free will has the last word. In fact, I would go as far as to say that the challenge of managing our freedom is the biggest problem but also the greatness of Western contemporary society.

It's not that in the past people were driven on by an all-pervading sense of self-sacrifice. It's not that our forebears were motivated by the thrill of singing "Jack and Jill went up the hill" rather than going to a Massive Attack concert. They had no natural desire to put down their Cormac McCarthy novel and pick up some Hans Christian Andersen fairy tales. Sometimes their will was tempered by social circumstances, at other times by the kids turning up. As far as I can tell, our generation is no longer very good at working out what is good and what is bad for us. The power to choose when and how many children to bring into the world, individuals destined for eternal life, is a power that can't be totally handed over to mere creatures. Being open—responsible but open—to what comes along is something that saves us. It saves our lives.

But at this point, I am going to stop talking about human nature and original sin and all the rest. Antonio doesn't share my views on such matters, and I have no desire to argue with him. (Finding another friend at this stage in life, a friend who can have me falling about laughing just by raising his eyebrow, is too much of a challenge. At my stage in life you keep the friends you've got!)

The point is, he is no longer engaged to Chiara, but he is engaged to someone else, and I place all my remaining hopes in his new fiancée. Whatever the propaganda machine might tell us about blurring the distinctions between the two sexes—calling father and mother parent one and parent two—it is women who are called to care for life, to show its beauty to men and to invite them to make the massive leap of faith. To have children today is a rare concept in the age of the exaltation of self. For instance, children compete against private property, such as iPods, desks, and Elizabeth Arden lipsticks. They also compete against technological domination. The genes of children can't be programmed like computers; otherwise, I would have removed the gluttony gene from my kids so that I wouldn't find cheese rind and curdled glasses of milk under the beds.

As for my desire to see more men displaying fatherly authority—an authority different from the mothers, with different roles, different attitudes, and different expertise—I have to say, I'm pretty disappointed. The propaganda machine that churns out a single, politically acceptable line is working hard in the opposite direction. Fathers are being asked, through everyday attitudes and also through those laws and customs that form any culture, to be variants on the mother, and so we are losing sight of the male/female polarity that constitutes the foundations of humanity.

I am consoled, however, by the fact that when I find myself saying these things—be it at conferences or in articles I write—there's always a "hurrah" that encourages me, mothers nodding in approval, and fathers expressing their gratitude. Marvelous, good dads, who, yes, sometimes forget they left their kid on the teeter-totter, take the wrong child to the doctor (it was the eldest who had the high temperature, not the youngest!), or nimbly overlook certain basic hygiene requirements ("Did you take a shower yesterday?" "No, Mom, you were at work and dad was looking after us."). But despite all this they are great fathers; fathers who have the courage to end things that need to be ended, to choose, to decide, to open the door when it's time for kids to leave, and to prepare a place for their return. You see, such men still exist—despite the propaganda.

CHAPTER 10

CRISTIANA

OR

I'VE SEEN THINGS THAT YOU "MEN" COULDN'T EVEN IMAGINE

Dear Cristiana,

How much time have you got? It's just that if you get me started talking about work and about the children, you'd better have four free hours and be very well disposed toward me. I will almost certainly get hysterical, begin to bore you, complain a lot, and become annoying. I may even burst into tears. Things will escalate all on their own, and I will end up suggesting that you change jobs and then emigrate, and finally with that moderation for which I am so well known, I'll be advising you to raze to the ground the whole country with Napalm bombs.

Shall we talk about our desks, which seem to have disappeared when we return from maternity leave

197

or about colleagues who consider us imbeciles and second-class workers? Or shall we discuss the fact that the idea of having it all is one colossal lie? Or maybe we could discuss the maternity pay in France or the incentives for part-time work in Holland, where, if you ask for it, the company is required to grant it to you. Or should we talk about all those Italian women who would give anything to work part time and instead have to leave their kids at a day care and walk away with a broken heart and tears in their eyes?

On all of the above, I am very well versed and ready for battle.

Soon you will be going back to work, and you don't know how you're going to organize your life. The first thing to do is forget people like Nancy Pelosi, who, on the day of the eighteenth birthday (and I stress *eighteenth*) of her fifth child (and I stress *fifth*), reentered the job market, not as a shop assistant in the neighborhood store, but as Speaker of the House of Representatives, thus becoming the highest-placed woman ever in the United States. They didn't tell her she was too old or that she had too many kids. So don't think about her as an example.

Italy is the country that has the lowest birthrate in the world. Here the world of work is set against mothers and therefore also against children.

This is just a fact. It's not that the world of work is closed to women. The problem is that women can't seem to change the world of work. Either you accept its rules, its rhythms, and its hours or you're out. Marginalized. The world of work doesn't care if, at home, you have a baby desperate for the mother's milk that he or she has a right to.

It doesn't matter if you have to correct homework, listen, console, get the children to bed, and change diapers, and even though you could condense the same amount of work as you've always done into less time by avoiding some of the things that your college colleagues do—playing around on the computer, chatting, making phone calls, and spending a bit of time at the coffee machine—because you are needed at home, none of that matters.

Neither does it matter that bringing up the kids has taught you to do three things at once, allowing you to manage perfectly well at work, doing things faster than before. After having had to deal with projectile vomit, spots on the forehead, and overnight convulsions, you can cope with anything.

Alas, we are not in Norway, where even a proabortion prime minister like Gro Harlem Brundtland came to realize that it was a good idea to have business meetings at eight o'clock in the morning so that women could hurry along and make the appointment after dropping the kids off at preschool. By four o'clock, the whole family is home—and I'm not talking about postal workers only; I mean all state employees, male and female.

Here in Italy, we women study for years, hoping we will be able to have it all—career and children—but it's not possible. Or rather it's not possible except for a few rare cases of professions that are marvelously flexible, manageable, and adaptable to the various seasons in the life of a mother and her children.

There are also those cases where there is an enlightened boss, like my own dear Ilda Bartolini, with whom I used to have very lively debates about abortion and feminism (lively to the point of throwing things!) but who understood the needs of a mother who was always about to head off on an assignment with a sandwich in her handbag—think of a Fendi purse mixed with a cold cuts smell. She recognized the needs of this particular mom who kept in her diary return tickets for trips that must have been something of a world record: Palermo for almost two hours, Stockholm for six hours, and Berlin for four hours. No trips around the city; no lunch at Vienna's most expensive restaurant as a guest of the local press office. All that mattered was that I was home with the interview in the can and in time for the karate lesson or the second day of antibiotics.

But Ilda died, and we, her "girls," miss her in so many ways, not least because she knew how to run the office as only a woman can. All of us have benefited, knowing how to use our talent for seeing the best in situations, fitting things in, going without food and drink, writing an article in an airport lounge, sketching out interview questions on the couch in the children's clinic, and catching up with the press preview while watching *Bambi*.

Ilda has gone and her girls have grown up, and along the way we've had to find a way to cope: Either our children don't get the attention they need (and to which they have a right) or we find ourselves outflanked at work by anyone who shows the slightest dedication and bit of teamwork.

No one is saying that a working mom should have supernatural powers, that she should be able to see to every detail, sending her kids to parties bearing home-baked cakes (I always seem to find myself asked to provide drinks or junk food, like chips—my fame as a culinary disaster area clearly precedes me). No one expects our kids to turn up with frog masks hand-stitched in the middle of the night by an expert maternal seamstress or imagines that we should be arranging the cultural development of our little darlings by introducing them to the joys of literature and art through regular visits to the library and museum exhibitions.

But a mom who works outside the home has to be able to be present for her kids and listen to them when they need her. Something's not right if her standard reply is, "OK, but not now. I'm busy at the moment," because her every waking moment is devoted to providing for the physical survival of her offspring. (The same offspring who can go to the party with a cake bought in the supermarket with its wrapping removed, thus making it look a bit like a homemade effort.) Her kids have to know that when they need her, she will be there and is not just a voice at the end of a cell phone. They should be able to feel their mom's hands holding them, even if they are worked to the bone.

While we're waiting in line to speak to the teachers at the parent-teacher conference, moms chat among themselves. They compare households; they even compare husbands: Mine gets in the groceries. Mine doesn't, but he did remember our anniversary. Mine even noticed last month that I had been to the hairdresser. Really? Really?? But on one thing all the moms agree: Working moms are all shattered by their double role. They are seen washing on the balcony after midnight, greeting each other in the wee hours of the night from one balcony to another. They're always short of time, especially time for themselves, which is always the first thing they go without. And yet we continue to speak about going out to work as a "conquest."

"Lavinia, what a lovely drawing. Who is this?" I said a month or so ago to my daughter, an implacable observer of everything that happens in our house.

"It's you, Mom."

"So why did you draw me with a banana on my head?"

"It's not a banana. That's your hair. That's what it's like, brown underneath and yellow on top."

My roots. Maybe it is time to get my hair done again; it's clearly time for my biannual visit to the stylist.

But that's it. We turn a blind eye or maybe two blind eyes to the need to spend a little time on ourselves but never fail to suffer for the time we're forced to rob from our children.

Among all the women in that line waiting to see the teacher at the parent-teacher conference— managers, engineers, accountants—there wasn't one who wouldn't have happily cut back on work commitments, those work commitments that we struggled to achieve but that have sometimes turned into a kind of prison for us, even when our jobs are noble and maybe even rewarding and well paid.

Dear Cristina, I'm sorry not to be able to provide you with a happier accompaniment as you go back to work. But let me tell you this: You'll manage just fine! You'll find your own way of doing things at your own rhythm and you'll keep the whole show on the road. Even if I don't feed you the old line about "quality over quantity" when it comes to spending time with the kids, it is true that quality does matter.

When I was freelancing and I was alternating between periods as a homemaker and periods as a working journalist, I realized that to really be part of kids' lives, it wasn't enough just to be physically present. It was complicated because the nanny was also part time, and when I was at home, I needed her for fewer hours a week. I remember I used to spend almost all my time tidying up: A house can turn into a black hole that endlessly swallows up your time. On the other hand, during the periods when I was working, I pretended not to notice the yogurt stains decorating the carpet so I could spend all my energies on the kids. I found myself ignoring mountains of clothes waiting to be ironed so I could take aspiring young art experts to the Vatican Museums, only to discover that "the Vatican mummy collection is better than the Sistine Chapel"—but hey, who cares? At least they got to see the museums and took something away from the visit.

You'll find that it's the same for you. You'll find a way to hold down your job, create a traffic jam with toy cars, prepare the dinner, and listen to the full story of a massive tiff between two little best friends.

Sure, you'll always be too much of a geologist to be a real mom and too much of a real mom to be a geologist. You'll either be late handing in the report or cause a public relations nightmare with your kids. You'll be distracted as you type on your laptop while breastfeeding, failing to live up to the latest weaning theories (frozen soups from the packet for your baby rather than home-produced puree of zucchini). And all that happens because you have to get to a meeting on time. You'll always feel a bit out of it, in whichever setting you find yourself, a bit like my friend Paolo, who is a massage therapist for soccer teams and never knows whether to be in or out of the official team photo each year, not sure if he is really part of the squad, and if he is, standing awkwardly for the picture with a tense smile on his lips.

Be brave! Dive right back in there, and if you need a life vest, I'm right here!
C

Is it a good thing for women to work? This is one of the few questions I just wouldn't know how to answer. That's despite the fact that I am usually so black and white about issues. I normally go around with a metaphorical cutlass between my teeth, driving wedges between good and evil, right and wrong, truth and falsehood in my own life and, God forgive me, in other people's lives, too. I am so nonmulticultural and nonecumenical—the exact opposite of the sower of doubt.

But in this case, the question is rather more complex, and so I will try in my answer to be as clear and accurate as I possibly can. Let's put it like this: A woman can't work as much as a man if she has children, nor can she work in the same way as a man even if she doesn't have children.

A woman's work should be capable of being adapted to the particular phase of life of the people the woman cares for and should always bear the hallmark of welcome.

It's not that I don't realize that what I am saying is "out of line"—I do! But I am comforted by the fact that it represents the thoughts of many real women that I know, who don't write books or run campaigns but who get on with their lives. And there are many of them.

The question we have to ask ourselves is this: What is best for my children, my family, and the people who rely on me? The answer to this question is more important than all others. It comes before any discussion of self-fulfillment—which is usually considered sacrosanct but comes later. It is more important than having free time, economic independence, and an education and career.

With the cutlass between my teeth, I dare to affirm that a child, in the first three years of life, needs more or less a mother's constant presence. Certainly, the child needs absences to be kept to a minimum, and the time a mother spends away from the child should not be greater than the time spent with the child. In the first year of life, even a blind man could see that a baby wants, quite rightly, to be with his or her mommy. A society that doesn't acknowledge this is a society that maltreats its children. They can put forward all the economic and organizational excuses they want, but they should be clear that these are excuses that are being used to trample on the rights of the most vulnerable.

I can't claim to have been a good example in my own life. With my first two children, I wasn't able to get much time off work, causing me stomachaches, an anxious heart, and endlessly dripping breast pads! I am not convinced that leaving your kids in a daycare or even with their marvelous grandparents is any kind of emancipation. I'm not convinced that it's any great boon to leave your kids at school all day long, not being able to help them with their homework, leaving them in the hands of teachers, who, even if you are lucky and the teachers are great, you can't choose. I'm not convinced that paying such a high price to enter the vicious circle of production and consumption is emancipation. Equally, I'm not sure that dividing equally all the housework with the father, mixing up roles, and causing heartache on both sides is emancipation. I suspect that such heartache has a lot to do with many relationship crises.

There are jobs and there are *jobs*. I recognize that. Often a job is just a way of making money, an indispensable necessity to allow a decent standard of living. If that's the case, then surely it's time to look at the big picture again? If, in the past, one salary was enough, and now two are required, that surely means that the employer is hiring two workers and paying one wage, right? Some intelligent economist needs to help me get my head around a few things! But I also wonder, would we be lowering our quality of life if we were to eliminate certain "essential" things that in the past would have been regarded as luxuries? Or is it maybe that the basic essentials—housing costs, especially— now cost so much that two salaries are needed to cover them when one would have been enough in the past?

There are other jobs, though, which are taken on mainly to provide satisfaction and to improve living standards, and I sense they are more common than we might think. In such cases, slowing down on the career treadmill when the kids come along is a duty, and those who refuse to do so are simply being selfish, and I use that word advisedly.

I recognize that it's not an easy choice, because for some reason we tend to regard work outside the home as being somehow more worthy than work in the house. Maybe because official certificates of recognition are a bit harder to come by at home and there's the danger of being taken for granted. Let's admit it—the prizes for working in the home are not exactly sparkling, and when you do get some kind of recognition, you have to store it away and preserve it to make up for the times you find yourself regarded more as a domestic appliance than a domestic goddess! Domestic appliances don't get much recognition. Not many people thank the washing machine at the end of its cycle.

"Bernardo, are you glad that Mom's moving to a different department, one that she likes better?"

"What does it matter to me? It doesn't change anything in my life. Don't you know the golden rule? Everyone is happy for himself."

"That doesn't sound a very good rule to me," I gasp, as I realize how singularly unsuccessful I have been in teaching my son the basics of Christian charity, let alone the bare essentials of filial love.

"In my new office, I'm going to be closer to the snack machine."

"In that case, I'm happy. Because when I come in to see you next time, I won't have to climb all those stairs to get a chocolate bar."

Despite the blows to maternal self-esteem, I try to use my intelligence to educate the kids (in vain, obviously!) just as much as I use it at work, where, it must be said, it's much less of a struggle.

I know a lovely mom of six kids. She has a degree in philosophy but was very happy to stay at home when the children came along. I also know another lovely mom of six kids who was very happy to keep on working as a psychiatrist when the children arrived. Maybe the time has come to examine again the traditional counterbalance between satisfaction and renunciation now that we have won the right to work and staying at home is no longer an obligation. Nowadays, it's a choice that can be made freely—joyfully, even—without any loss of self-esteem.

I think we also have to recognize that there are different kinds of women. There are some women forced to go to work while deep down, their heart beats for that tiny bundle of joy who has come into their lives, and there are others who will never give up their economic independence or their free time or ability to organize their lives, even when they are as rich as they can be. There are women who go to work to relax and pretend to have to work longer hours to avoid going home and fighting with the kids. There are some women who send the four-month-old baby to a preschool all day even when they only work part time in the afternoons, just so they can leave the morning free to go to the gym to firm up their buttocks. There are women who, without their work, would lose their sense of identity and would no longer be recognized socially or feel fulfilled.

Finally, there are jobs where you can make a worthwhile contribution even outside your own family circle. We women can do so much to improve the work industry: We can create hospitals where there is more compassion, newspapers that are less vacuous, courtrooms that are more efficient, schools that are more stimulating, and offices that work more efficiently. It's essential to try to improve working conditions. But in all of this, we have to remember that our first duty is to our husbands and children.

We have struggled hard to get to this stage; it has been a long battle. Let's not forget that it was only in the 1960s when Amintore Fanfani was prime minister of Italy and our government abolished the law that allowed employers to make women redundant when they got married and therefore risked becoming pregnant.

The issue is how to resolve these freedoms. It was an issue then, and it is still an issue. Is some kind of synthesis possible? I don't know.

Work, as far as I'm concerned, should be something that's flexible and amendable all through life. To take just one example, it should be possible to take a certain amount of years off, depending on two conditions. Even writing this makes me laugh because it is just so farfetched.

The first condition is that there should be decent family allowances. They shouldn't be seen as handouts and shouldn't require keen parents to live in utter squalor to qualify.

I often wonder, for example, why they don't use some of the money reclaimed from the great sea of tax evaders, given that a well-raised child will respect the rules and do his or her duty, even when it comes to paying taxes.

The second condition is that there employers should offer mothers their jobs after the time off instead of being sent to clean sewers or pressed into service as office photocopiers.

"You are asking for too much," I'm told by my colleagues who don't have children. Maybe they're right. If wanting to work and raise children is too much, then yes, I am asking for too much.

But many people believe that *our* children are *our* business, to put it crudely, and that belief might be shared by those who think that mothers whose minds are on their children are hopeless in the workplace.

But if, on the other hand, we recognize that children are a good for the whole of society—not only because they will pay our pensions and the like but because they will be the ones who will leave their mark on the world of the future in which we will live—then it makes sense to help and support those parents who want to dedicate themselves to their children's education.

Having a stay-at-home mom doesn't guarantee any successful outcome, of course. We could all cite examples of moms who were always around for their kids but were always useless and even damaging to their development. Indeed, if anyone has the recipe for successful child rearing, could they please let me have it?

Having said that, it can't be helpful to always delegate, always leave the kids in someone else's care, and always be too busy to spend time with them. Time is the very thing you need in order to manifest your love for them. You need to spend time with them to teach them how to reason, to stimulate their curiosity, to enthuse them, and to accompany them as they set their sights high. I don't have any magic formula for how you achieve all that, but you certainly don't achieve it by not being around.

My ideal would be to retire for ten years at this stage of my life and give back to my employer and to society ten years of work when I am sixty. The next time the Secretary of Labor is within range, I will suggest it to him. I can imagine how delighted his reaction will be!

Right now I am chronically tired and fall asleep on any surface on which I can lay down my aching limbs. But when I'm sixty, if I live that long, I will have to invent something to do to pretend that I still have a role. My husband fears that I will become unbearably hyperactive as a pensioner. He thinks I might go crazy and buy an RV and drive around the world to fill my time like the newly retired Jack Nicholson in the most depressing film of the decade, *About Schmidt*.

Would it not be better to have some time now, at a time when I would need to be able to work during every resting hour just to keep up with all my responsibilities?

Every night for the last 12 years, as I go to bed far too late, with a ton of things on my mind (ironing, kids' backpacks, bills, and all the things I have to read), I announce to my husband that the following morning, I'm going to get up at 6:00 a.m.—that is, four hours later. I tell him that I will go to the austere Monastic Mass at 6:20 a.m., then I will go for a bracing run around the walls of Rome for half an hour. I'll come home, put the croissants in the oven, take a shower, and then, after a quick leaf through the newspapers, I'll wake everyone else in the house with a cheerful chorus of "Rise and shine."

I think I have managed it once. Once in 12 years. The sad truth is that my husband often has to push me off the bed with his feet when I am already late for the first basic task of getting the kids to school on time. Thus, I'm running an hour and a half late before I've even leave the house.

So while I wait for the law to be changed to allow me to draw my pension 25 years early, I have to try to compromise and indulge in a bit of damage control, cutting short my plans and accepting my tendency to be late. Thus, I try not to flop on the desk after spending a night holding damp cloths to fevered brows. Thus, I try to appear intelligent and knowledgeable when I haven't a clue what the boss is talking about— about *that* event that happened last night, which everyone is talking about and discussing because it was the top story on the national news and dominated the prime time talk shows. I desperately try to work out what has happened without revealing my ignorance—has Obama died or has China decided to call in all its credit and bring down the world economy? I fumble in the dark because at eight o'clock the night before, I wasn't watching the evening news. I was watching cartoons or cleaning up spat-out semolina.

Every time the issue of flexibility for working moms is discussed in newspaper articles or in public debate, the talk is always of building more preschools, never about real flexibility in work practices. Building even more preschools to leave your three-month-old baby is not the kind of help working mothers need. Equal opportunities would really be promoted by allowing a mother to stay off work to look after her young children rather than killing herself both in the home and outside the home, leaving her hungry baby in the hands of someone else.

It seems clear to me, therefore, that women cannot work the same way that men do; they have to find their own way, one that is designed around them and fits their needs. It's not right to force people to choose all the time—you need to accept the rules, the timetable, and the ways of male colleagues and forget everything that's happening at home. If not, you're out!

My friends tell me that in many offices, the amount of time they spend in front of the computer is the main consideration, even if they are surfing the Internet, playing solitaire, reading horoscopes, writing distant relatives and unlikely friends, or taking endless trips to the vending machine to sample cans of liquids with worrying names but that are a distant relative of tea. Anything goes as long as they don't leave the office until late in the evening, sitting up straight, letting everyone see they are there and indispensable, showing that without their presence, the company would collapse.

A woman with a thousand things to do at home will always try, where possible, to concentrate on her work and cut out any time-wasting activities so she can get home earlier. It's just that for some perverse reason that my poor mind is incapable of comprehending, this ability to do the same amount of work in a shorter space of time is not considered an attribute but a limitation. With that logic, prevailing women are always going to suffer.

As long as working arrangements continue as they are, failing to integrate family life and working life, lacking in flexibility and intelligence, and ignoring the interests of those very children that they are always boasting that they want to protect but that they really don't care about, women will be obliged to pay a very high price on the altar of work sacrifice or give up and walk away.

That would be a shame because we are good and we have something to offer. You only have to look at the difference between boys and girls at school. From a strictly educational point of view, it's no contest. The girls beat their classmates by a mile. Of course, it's also true that school exam results aren't the be all and end all of everything. The biographies of geniuses are full of stories of dull teachers who failed to spot that fleeting quality of intelligence.

But the fact remains that from preschool to college level, girls come out on top, they are more diligent and quicker to finish their studies. So I wonder when they are overtaken? At which precise point on the road between the first day of elementary school and the presidency of the International Monetary Fund do females lose all their intelligence, skill, and capacity to work? How is it that school teachers find girls do better than boys but those same girls never make it onto the boards of powerful institutions? At what point in their development does their intelligence become so obscured that it prevents them from achieving positions that matter in the centers of real power—namely, economic power?

It's clearly not a *skills* problem but a *power* problem. Those who reach positions of power must be reliable and trusted to make decisions based on the internal logic of that power, which must be maintained and guaranteed. That's why women don't make it. Women are by nature welcoming, and the command structure follows quite a different logic. It's not designed for us. Power sought as a means of self-affirmation doesn't interest most women.

But blaming others, even though it's a pretty widespread attitude, is actually a sign of immaturity. And it's also boring.

We women should give up the logic of complaint and take cognizance of the fact that we are *different*. It's not a conspiracy and it's not about oppression; rather, it's that we are made for a different type of power. When we obtain it, we should see it as a responsibility to be exercised carefully, as a mother would exercise it. Not for us women is the role of the supreme allied commander who decides all things for all people but rather the role of the intelligent person who understands what those people for whom we are responsible can do and gives everyone their place.

Women know how to handle people, difficult situations, and, of course, emergencies. I like those bumper stickers that you see on minivans that read, "I can manage any crisis: I have children." Of course women can handle any crisis. Women can see forward, backward, and all around with their eyes, their ears, their hands, and their nose.

We are well able to operate on several fronts at once, quickly resolving problems at work without forgetting what's happening at home. We're not fazed at all by a film crew that doesn't show up, an airline strike, or shadowing a high-ranking politician for the day. One problem at a time is nothing to us. We can put up with tiredness and pain better than men, as anyone will testify who has ever seen a man with a high temperature of 99.5 degrees dictating his last will and testament.

Despite that, though, we are not made for power grabbing. Those women who do obtain it are often angry because they may be going against their instincts, becoming anxious and aggressive. And if, on the one hand, they renounce elements of their own profound femininity—sweetness, openness—on the other hand, they reclaim it by incarnating its worst stereotypes. They can become irascible, emotional, and capable of things most men wouldn't even dream of.

This is the doubt that gnaws at us and that we never really find an answer to—coffee breaks are too short or the phone calls when cooking breaded chicken (that specialty of the working mother) aren't long enough. Do people become bad when they reach positions of power, or do they reach positions of power because they were bad in the first place?

Three Years Later . . .

Cristiana left her job as a university researcher when she realized that she was earning slightly less than her nanny, who was looking after the baby for five hours a day while she was at college. Cristiana did the rest of her work at night when the nanny presumably could allow herself the luxury of sleep.

To the seventy-second person who said to her, "It's an investment for the future," she delivered a right hook and then decided to give up! As investments go, this one was performing pretty badly. It seemed clear that not long hence, her contract wouldn't be renewed and she would never get a promotion to the top job. The two other candidates for the role didn't have any children. For them it was a pleasure to go for an aperitif with the professor at seven o'clock at night—for Cristiana, that is the sacred hour of the fish stick, which has been the culinary savior of many working mothers.

The others were able to accompany him to the conference: nothing untoward, all quite legitimate, but it left them at a definite advantage over Cristiana, for whom it was impossible to show enthusiasm for the latest piece of MIT research late into the night. At that hour we moms are struggling against sleep, sitting on a little pink chair twelve inches off the ground, reading *The Little Mermaid*, and strongly tempted to reveal that the foolish creature in Andersen's story commits suicide. Enough!

No more reading! She's dead! Let's switch off the light and get used to the fact that life is not a Disney cartoon and you'd better get some sleep, because tomorrow you've got a hard day ahead.

Nowadays, Cristiana works—on a short-term contract, obviously—for a distance-learning college, so she can do much of her work from home, going into the office only to record lessons and for exams. The rest of the time, she organizes herself as best she can—in other words, badly. For many women, asking for the help they need and taking the required time, even if they need to for work, is very difficult. The fact that I am writing these words at four o'clock in the morning says a lot.

If I think of ten good friends of mine, I realize that each one of them has found her own very personal way to reconcile all the demands placed on her. Some have sought part-time work, some have left work, some stay on in their jobs after having hired three nannies and enrolled the help of three able grandparents. Some survive only by having their children full time in childcare while getting up at five o'clock in the morning to do the ironing. If you meet one friend of mine and try to say hello, you notice she is looking at a fixed point behind your head (she's visualizing the next thing on her "to do" list), and if you find her one day, lying stone dead on the steps of the catechism class, you'll know you should have intervened sooner! Others survive by changing jobs or by working from home. All of them face a huge struggle to keep the family-work show on the road. Even if they appear to be coping and seem to have found a reasonable balance, the chances are that they will have learned to live in a state of perpetual lateness. They will be the ones who have to beg the high school secretary to delay the graduation ceremony for a day, the ones who have to plead with the receptionist for a slot to see the dermatologist and then have to put up with disapproving stares because they are a full seven months late for the aforementioned checkup, and the ones who have to pretend that they know there has been a substitute math teacher for the last three weeks.

And these are only the things they have to pretend to know wearing their *mom's* hat. Because wearing their *employee's* hat, there are a range of other things they have to pretend to be up to date with—the big news this month, the important meeting, the extraordinary announcement, and the chat in the corridors that they haven't the slightest clue about (but it's all right as long as they refer to it in a manner that's part knowledgeable and part conspiratorial).

None of this is the result of some male plot. It's just the way things are. We simply can't control everything the way we would like, and those who have the luxury of choosing between staying at home or going out to work are becoming fewer and fewer. Those who have a job hang on to it. What's the answer? I think you have to try to answer it in your own way, but be aware that there is no *right* answer. There is no formula to make everything work *perfectly* (there it is again, that insidious word that is a woman's worst enemy).

I suggest, though, that you form pacts of steel with other friends-in-need so as to create a solid support network that you can rely on. I'm late handing this in, can I leave my three kids with you for the next two afternoons? I'll look after your daughter the day you move to a new house. I'll be there at the school gates; there's no need to keep a shotgun on the back seat of the car to fire just like they do in the movie *Falling Down* if the highway is gridlocked. Fear not—if you're late, your son won't be left standing on the school steps like a sad little soul. A squadron of reservist moms will be called up to save him, because if each of us clone ourselves seven or eight times over, then we'll definitely manage.

Chapter 11

Marta

Or

We're Bigger than You and It's Our House

Dear Marta,

I wasn't able to call you earlier, and it's now so late at night I'd better not. All the better for you, as you are a member of my "emergency friends" team to be called upon when necessary.

You are a little bit older than me, much wiser, and infinitely more balanced than I am, with the gifts of foresight and good sense, which are totally lacking in yours truly.

Your children are older than mine, you see things from a better perspective, and the pain you've endured in your life and accepted has made you a better person—good, gentle, and so reassuring. As Virgil puts it, "Non ignara mali, miseris succurrere discis"—no

218

stranger to misfortune yourself, you have learned to relieve the sufferings of others.

Earlier, if I had been able, I would have inflicted a phone call on you—the kind that is like getting the car serviced or having your temperature taken.

My husband always says that the phrase "Come stai?" (how are you?) in Italian is a social greeting or a courtesy. If someone asks you this question, which is nothing more than a stock phrase—so says the bear who passes for my husband—it does not mean that the person has a profound curiosity to discover where you are in your existential journey through life. The unsuspecting interlocutor does not really want you to lay before him the latest entry in your diary.

In reply, I tell him that I can't understand how he can spend days and nights with colleagues while on work trips away from home, grunting only to exchange those meager details of information that are absolutely essential to survival, such as the latest on the transfer market in the world of soccer and the address of the restaurant where the next meal will be eaten. Men can spend a week together in Malaysia and return home with absolutely no news, no gossip to share.

"How is your colleague? Is he happy? Is he in love? Are they getting married?"

"I don't know. I never asked him."

Such absence of basic information is incomprehensible to me and to those of us who tend to go in for major sharing sessions while waiting in line with our children for the swings in the playground. We like to get right to the heart of things.

Anyway, if I had called you and if you had said, "How are you?" I would have been off like a shot. I would have begun by rattling off all my latest doubts about the education system. I am becoming ever more convinced that I may be at the point of becoming world champion screw up. I take a few steps back, take a deep breath, and run for it . . . faster and faster. I think about it. I prepare myself. This time I won't get it wrong. This time I have prepared well . . . and oops. Another mistake.

I console myself with the thought that it's better to be the champion of high-level mistakes than long-distance mistakes. Not persevering—that would be a diabolical error. We have to correct ourselves, ask forgiveness sometimes, and above all, have confidence in He who entrusted these children to us, believing in us more than we believe in Him, and more, perhaps, than we believe in ourselves.

But back to tonight. Tonight there will be no phone call. What we need is a catch-up course on contemporary (sub)culture.

Recently at home we threw ourselves into a television miniseries—one of those series where the characters appear to have been crafted with all the subtlety of a blunt pickaxe. The grumpy guy with the heart of gold, the rascal, the pretty young woman—the whole thing shot and edited with about the same level of sophistication and skill as a First Communion video. To be fair to the bosses of the television channel who would have spent pots of money on it, I should say that my kids quite enjoyed it. It was ideal for elementary school kids who, as everybody knows, quickly want to know who are the good guys and whose side they should be on.

I decided to let the big ones watch a bit of television while two friends of my younger son were over to play—that's the son who is a taciturn eight-year-old philosopher. They were out in the garden—or rather, in the space that you haven't seen yet but that you, like me, would struggle to call a garden. Both of us have a different concept of a garden, having grown up in Umbria surrounded by the rolling hills that serve as background to those paintings of Our Lady by Perugino. Here, on the other hand, all you can see over the hedge is smelly and noisy cars and scooters. Despite all that, it's a space that in Rome, in the heart of the San Giovanni quarter, is really unusual and precious, so much so that it has become a mecca for the kids' friends.

Maybe it's because when they are out there, they enjoy a bit of freedom from adult supervision, since I prefer to leave them alone, adopting your approach— a kind of affectionate turning of a blind eye. I intervene only when I see blood flowing or works of art smashed to pieces.

Every now and then, I see a slightly improper use of water guns and hear shouted exchanges that would not be exactly models of good taste with kids from the buildings in the neighborhood, inelegantly described on one occasion as "the second-floor dummies." But I don't let on, remembering our own childhood games when, without parental intervention, we pretty much learned how to live. Anyhow, during one of these "free" periods, the gang of little friends went up to a woman who was passing by on the other side of the hedge.

"What's your name?"

"Barbara."

"Do you know that I am the son of somebody famous? I'm the son of Massimo Boldi," said our guest who wanted to make a big impression on the lady. (Massimo Boldi is an Italian stand-up comedian and actor.)

"I'm the son of Christian De Sica," announced another of them. (Christian De Sica is an actor often seen in Italian television and films.)

My own son Bernardo couldn't think of any "famous" person to impress the passerby. The only thing that came to mind was "I am the son of Lillo!" (Lillo is one-half of a comic duo, Lillo e Greg.)

He had picked this up because every now and again, we listen to the duo's radio show. The kids' favorite character on the show is called NormalMan—an indolent, uneducated, and fearsome character who acquires magical powers and becomes normal. Thus, he manages to carry out ordinary (on reflection, maybe make that extraordinary) tasks like helping old ladies with their shopping.

Alas, nearly all the famous people our kids know about are dead and have been for a while: Charlie Chaplin, the Marx Brothers—even Huckleberry Finn is not in great health these days.

It's our fault, I fear. Our eldest child wants to start a band called Thirty Too Lates, for those born thirty years too late. He's an unusually aware boy who grew up with *Peanuts* cartoons, the animation of Bruno Bozzetto and the *Giornalino di Gian Burrasca* (an adventure story from 1907 that was made into a hit television series in Italy in the 1960s).

To give you an idea, in his language, the phrase "May I have a glass of water?" comes out as "I need beer and new information." "I'm going to the bathroom" is rendered as "I'm in a meeting in the Oval Office." And when he is going on a journey, after saying a prayer, the formula recited is, "We've got a full tank, half a pack of cigarettes, it's dark, and all six of us are wearing sunglasses. Go!"

Only now, for the first time ever, do I feel guilty about having kept the kids so far away from contemporary culture. This is one of the doubts that has assailed me since they entered the preadolescent stage.

How much do you require to be *in* the world but not *of* the world? In practical terms, is there anything worth watching on television? Is it enough to see only decent films to avoid becoming a social misfit? I only say that because I know that you're not one of those fanatical parents who would smash any screen that came between your little darlings and their daily dose of politically correct games.

On the other hand, film was the only art form that came into existence in the twentieth century, and even if I say so with a hefty dose of caution (I have my doubts about the artistic merits of the *Incredible Hulk*), movies are surely worth getting into.

It's not necessarily a sign of great intelligence to do what I did though. When I got engaged, I had seen just two films: *Cinderella* and *When Harry Met Sally*—though it has to be said, I had seen both about 25 times each.

By way of payback, I married a film editor. In the early days, he tried to give me a crash course to make up for my inadequacies. He lent me VHS tapes (that's how long ago it was), and he used to call me at home:

"Are you watching the Bergman film?"

"Yes, of course."

"So what's that sound I'm hearing? Is that running water?"

"I'm washing the dishes."

"But you can't do that!" he would shout into my ear down the telephone line. "You can't watch Kubrick, Bergman—not even Billy Wilder or Cameron Crowe—while you're washing the dishes!"

I have to say, I still wash dishes while watching a movie—especially given that if I sit down to watch a movie, I inevitably fall asleep.

In the everyday life of a parent, as you know much better than me, there is an infinite series of decisions to be taken, and it's best to have a clear and well-argued position on potential problems before they arise. That way, when you get inundated with the barrage of "Can I get . . . ?" questions (Can I get sweets, ice cream, chips, and so on? They never ask for beetroot puree, strangely enough!) or the "Can I . . ."? questions (Can I play with the PlayStation, jump off the table, and so on? They never ask to do homework, obviously!), you know exactly how to respond. And you have to seem very much in command of the situation:

"Yes, you *must* have a bath—you simply *must*" is more effective than trying to explain it all (describing the marvelous fruits of perfect hygiene to a little one has very little impact).

Similarly, you shouldn't make up the shopping list when you are already in the supermarket or the awful shopping mall. You have to be strong, firm though flexible, and on guard as my children know only too well. They use that knowledge in clever ways, like asking me for things when I am on the phone and my defenses are lowered.

Some standoffs have been avoided by setting aside specific days when the PlayStation can be brought out. They can have it two days a week. On the other days there's no point in asking and no point in trying to take advantage of lowered levels of awareness on the part of the parents.

Decisions, decisions, decisions . . . they lurk around every corner, whatever age the children are. They begin right at the start: how to get them to sleep, how much to hold them, when to let them into your bed, how to potty train them, how to wean them off pacifiers and bottles. Finding the right balance between firmness and sweetness and between the general rule and the particular exception can sometimes seem a major task.

Homework, for example, is a daily Calvary in our house. "You're worse than the teacher," the kids say to me. They are always on the lookout for the maximum result from the minimum effort. Maybe they are inspired by the ascetical "Ne quid nimis" (nothing in excess) of St. Benedict's rule or, more likely, by "The Bare Necessities," Baloo the Bear's song in *The Jungle Book*. They like to consider themselves in conformity with the great tradition of western monasticism when they decide to forget all that stuff about cutting out leaves, memorizing dates, and rote learning the times tables.

If education is all about setting sail toward autonomy, is it better to leave them alone or glue them to the desk and chair? I know freedom worked for Alfieri (Vittorio Alfieri was an eighteenth-century writer considered the father of Italian tragedy), but he loved learning. We have to work with our own kids who are smart but not used to sweating blood over their studies, bombarded as they are with ever-changing stimuli. They are certainly not helped by a school system that seems to believe that teaching kids to read, write, and count is too little. Instead of introducing hyper-stimulated youngsters who seem utterly incapable of concentration to the joys of textual analysis, logic, and history, the educationalists seem to feel the need (despite the heroic efforts of some good teachers with a real desire to work) to offer courses in dance, cricket, and—I kid you not—"tasting"!

In this land of no rules, when the prevailing culture encourages people to grab what they can and when our own comfort is exalted, corruption is a lifestyle option, and our own choices are to be defended at all costs, don't you ever feel tempted to tell kids the truth about how things really are? They have to understand very clearly the importance of respecting the rules, but they also have to know how to protect themselves. We know that one day we will have to give an account of ourselves and our lives to God, and I tell myself that we should not be afraid of that. But even so—as well as being as innocent as doves, we need to be as wise as serpents. How do you get from reading *Milo Goes to*

Kindergarten to reading the menu of cynicism and scandal in the daily newspapers?

To make matters worse, my family lives in the place that, better than any other, sums up Italy's national spirit: Rome. It is both a capital of disorder and a capital of beauty, where just a few yards apart, you can find the sublime and the squalid, apparently ignoring each other. Here you find people living shoulder to shoulder, some who are kind, others who are unspeakably rude. On the one hand, there are the gentlemen from the bar who climb over the fence to fetch your son's beloved leather ball and, on the other, the beastly creature who parks in the handicapped space and stops you from getting past with your stroller.

What do you do in such cases? Teach your kids to be stubbornly law abiding in all circumstances? To drive around the block six times looking for a parking space? Or should you just leave the car carelessly double-parked, using the traditional Roman phrase "C'ho r' pupo"—"I've got a baby with me." When I hear that excuse, I feel like saying, "I have a family, too, but I wouldn't do that, even when I have all four with me and it's raining!"

And then among the many arguments I'll bore you with over the next 15 years or so, there will be the question to end all questions: How do we bring up children in the faith? How do we pass on what we know to be the truth while respecting the freedom of children growing up, a freedom that they rightly cherish? I've listened to an array of experiences from friends and acquaintances covering the whole spectrum of suggestions: every option from insisting on the daily rosary to leaving the kids in absolute freedom in all matters relating to religion. The "He'll go to communion when he wants" approach to faith.

I remember saying to you long ago, "I think I've got it wrong somewhere." It was at a time when the first child was still small and the list of errors had yet to grow exponentially with the passage of time and the increase in the size of the family. "Just as well," you responded. "What a bore it would be to be the perfect mother."

OK, my kids seem to be safe from the "perfect mother risk," and I have often clung to that answer when through tiredness, distraction, or inability to reason. At certain times, I have screamed at the wrong child or got too angry—I need to learn to overlook their terrible handwriting every so often, given that some of my best friends write in block capitals. At other times, I don't get cross enough maybe—with me, they only need to feign a headache and my stern tone melts like an ice cream cone.

"I have to be patient with him. This may be the last hug I'll ever give him." I go all sentimental while the would-be patient lies on the couch with an *Asterix* comic book, having set aside his homework.

But kids are much better at coping with our mistakes than we might think. When they are secure in knowing that they are loved and when the parents know more or less who they are and what they are doing, mistakes can always be fixed.

The Good News we are to proclaim makes no mention of our perfection, but speaks rather of the omnipotence of God—the *Todo Poderoso*, as you liked to say that time you got back from Santiago de Compostela in Spain. Maybe I need to speak a bit more often about all these things with Him and call you a bit less—what do you think?

A big hug and lots of gratitude,
C

Man is a prodigious creature. To bring new exemplars of this wonder into the world—or to adopt them—and bring them up is a fantastic task that will always be looked upon favorably by *the* Boss (the one in heaven). This knowledge gives us the daring to try out the enterprise, the courage to carry it forward, and the certainty of succeeding in it.

Man can't help being a special creature. The voice of Dave Matthews is one of the proofs of the existence of God, as are the writings of Philip Roth, in my humble opinion. Who else could have invented them?

But even the people I know, incredible though it may seem, have the same effect on me (sometimes, not always). And while I agree with the psychiatrist Franco Basaglia that, seen close-up, no one is normal, I also think that seen close-up, everyone has something special and precious about them. Being human is a great and good thing. I am one of those people who admire the passersby on the sidewalk, so you can imagine how beautiful and good and all the other positive adjectives you can think of I find my own children.

Those who are on the side of life—parents first and foremost—are on the side of the angels. May the force be with you, as Obi-Wan Kenobi and Yoda would say.

But then there's original sin—that tendency toward evil that the dominant culture would say can be curbed with good principles and good intentions but that, in reality, is a powerful and sometimes violent presence deep within us. We believe that we have been given the power to overcome it, but the whole of life is a struggle against it.

There you are. That's about it. Simple.

Things aren't really that complicated. The truth is as simple as the structure of DNA, a helix that constitutes reality in all its forms, or like photosynthesis, a mechanism that's so simple that even an elementary school kid can understand, yet despite its simplicity it gives the world life.

All that is required is that parents—apart from loving, and loving with all their heart (we can assume this to be the case, I think)—keep in mind a few key points, and they ask themselves and remind themselves where that little being they have brought into the world is headed.

This is the question that should come before all others. Based on that first answer, all the others will flow.

For example, it becomes clear that if education is seen as the path toward adulthood, it is vitally important to teach children to delay their own gratification and also to move the search for pleasure onto something greater than themselves. For me this chapter could end here. In these few points there's enough food for thought for a week's reflection.

Actually, I personally have been reflecting on these points for more than 12 years, and I find it an exhausting task. It's tiring right at the start when all you really want to do is lay your head on the pillow with a good book. It's tiring to teach, and it's tiring to convey it to children who are obviously totally dominated by the law of pleasure—the desire for everything here and now. It's tiring to convey the heartfelt love that we feel for our little ones without taking away from them that scrap of authoritative guidance that they expect from us.

When they grow up (I wonder when all those fiftysomethings I'm thinking of will ever grow up?), we will help them learn to see some of their desires in the context of the cross and evaluate them with intelligence and realism. Or rather that's what we should be doing. Here the conditional tense is required, ever since the therapists and analysts have legitimized the subconscious, granting it the new right to be fully indulged.

But that is another question, and not one for me really. I have no particular expertise in the field unless there is an honors degree available for empirical observation of one's fellow citizens.

As for kids, there can be no doubts. Small children are egotistical. Adorable but egotistical. Irresistible but tyrannical. Our task is to love them madly until love itself is awakened in their hearts.

"Mom is like a big tree who gives you all her fruits. No matter how many you ask for, she always finds you one." This was the bold verse that I found attached to my Mother's Day present last year. Which parent among us hasn't received at least one kindergarten masterpiece—paper ties, pen holders, and a variety of hideous items—which we jealously guard and (even worse) show off to each other and which proclaims loudly our parental pride?

Yet all this stuff is basically the fruit of the teacher's creativity. In reality the kids don't notice what we do, and rightly so. Take, for example, the situation where we are busy doing something: it doesn't even occur to them to ask if they can interrupt, because for them, we exist to respond to their needs. It's important to know this. It stops us asking ourselves where we went wrong that we produced such a little monster. There I am, heroically preparing the dinner with a fever that's going through the roof, trying not to faint on top of the breaded fish, when the little darling asks me to wear the Darth Vader costume because he has to act out the final scene in *Star Wars* as Luke Skywalker and he can't find anyone to play the bad guy. Children prefer not to contemplate the fact that mom might need to make a phone call or go to the bathroom, let alone eat. For them, mom is an extension of themselves—an extension whose own needs don't come in to the equation.

Yet even when it all seems to be a hopeless task, we have to have the courage to ask something of our children, to expect something from them. "The roots of education are bitter, but the fruit is sweet." (That's Aristotle's line, I don't use such a sententious tone.) The courage to ask something of them now seems to be inconceivable for many parents. Through some twisting together of cultural factors, the thought of children being discontent in any way has become an intolerable thought. Such discontent is to be eliminated from their horizons ASAP. This goes for any kind of "suffering," even the eminently healthy lesson of feeling frustrated at being told no.

Yet the word *no*, when pronounced with a certain tone and as an expression of logic, can actually be reassuring for children. (Yes, dear husband, I know that when I am tired, I tend to use the words *yes* and *no* interchangeably. You're right.) The word *no* can actually help them feel better. After the tantrum, if they haven't obtained whatever it was they were irrationally demanding, the truth is they feel reassured in a funny kind of way. My parents know what they are doing—so they think—and know what they are talking about. In this way the world that is so unknown to them and so new begins to make some kind of sense.

Chaos is to be avoided. Children starting out in life are searching for limits and clear boundaries just like a blind person seeks the reassurance of a wall. Living in total darkness—so says the psychiatrist Giuliana Ukmar—children are far more scared by emptiness than they are by the limits of the wall. The unknown is more frightening than the clear boundary.

That's the way it is, even though we would prefer a million times over to take on their suffering and pay the price for them. We have to learn to accept—painful though it is—the suffering of our child as he seeks out boundaries in growing up. You can't remove it from early childhood experience. Clearly we don't set out looking for suffering, but neither can we eliminate it. At this point the subtitles begin to roll across the screen announcing, "The author of such statements is very well versed in theory but has a little difficulty in putting the theory into practice."

I hereby nominate my friend Marta as Secretary of State for Implementation of the Program.

Obviously, even I know that kids can't live forever in a Disney-type world, in a land of theme parks, because that's not reality. Suffering does come along at some point in all our lives, and even my children have to learn from it, for it doesn't end there.

Nowadays, even the great traditional fables are purged of any reference to suffering to make them saccharine sweet. Even the classics. To not disturb the tranquility of the child, at the end of the story, the wolf and the hunter make peace. I swear I am not exaggerating. I recently came across a book of fables told in a proanimal do-gooder sort of tone, so that deep down, the wolf was actually a good guy! I recently overheard a conversation between grandparents at the park (who should have known better), who were bemoaning the fact that all the stories aimed at their grandchildren always had a bad guy or a dragon or some danger that could disturb the little darlings' tranquility.

I found myself wondering how they could have forgotten all the witches and demons that were so much a part of the traditional Italian fable and that nourished the imagination of children long before Winnie the Pooh. It struck me that the scary bits in certain folktales—the wolf who eats you up or the dragon who kills you—can have an unforeseen educational and reassuring effect: Children are calmed by seeing their secret fears written down, especially the fear of death—which is an illness we contract at birth.

They may be little, but they are not stupid. They know things, and they are intuitive. Sometimes things get a little confused, and the realization that life isn't a bowl of cherries and the thought of keeping that realization secret, of hiding it, can frighten them even more than speaking about it. Who knows what terrors lie in the unknown? Much better, surely, to say, "Yes there is suffering in the world, but we have the confidence to live."

The so-called education crisis derives from the fact that we don't know any more why we educate children. What do we educate them in if even their parents don't know why they're here and where they're going? If you take away the sense of awe in God's presence, how do you begin to educate? If you remove the notion of original sin and the need to strive for salvation, what does it mean to educate? If you take away heaven and hell—considered to be the ridiculous notions of little old women by intellectuals apart from Camillo Langone (an Italian journalist and writer)—what point is there is trying to win eternal life if you are no more than a contented particle, as certain newfangled theologies would have it?

In these circumstances, a new and vague idea of goodness has emerged, which all must try to exercise in a context of complete freedom.

"What do you think, son? What will we have for dinner tonight?"

"What do you want to do? Where do you want to go?"

"Do you want to go home since it's that time?"

Those questions are a sure-fire way of setting off an argument, a trial of strength, which ends up making the kids both exhausted and exhausting, annoyed and annoying. They push us to the limits to see how far they can get, while deep down they want us to declare "enough is enough" and draw a line under the issue.

I admit I have found myself in these negotiating situations myself. Marta scolded me about four separate examples. (Would this be the best moment to list my mistakes? Surely I don't have to expose myself to the scorn of the public.) Maybe those of us who are parents all make the same kind of mistakes: we are all nonexperts, at times crushed by a task that our generation, for the first time in history, sees as a choice, not a natural, almost unavoidable stage in life. It seems everything has to be reinvented, and it is hard when we have very few fixed points overhead by which to navigate our ship through life.

Yet because of this, children suffer. Having to choose too much when you are too young is too great a responsibility. It can paralyze children at an early age.

We risk being a generation of parents who have produced children without a future, without direction, without goals. In school, references to our faith have been removed even from the poems they learn at Christmas and Easter to avoid offending anyone. But wait a minute . . . what kind of feasts are Christmas and Easter? Why not eliminate them all together and just celebrate Halloween?

We are left with a kind of ecological biodegradable sugary glop mentality where we are taught to be nice to each and every living creature, man or beast alike, as though this was some kind of universal natural sentiment—and sometimes even placing the welfare of the animal above that of the human.

For those who don't believe in anything, people for whom suffering makes no sense, for whom it is not in any way redeemed and doesn't bear any fruit, it must be kept away from children at all costs. There must be no frustration in their lives, no displeasure.

In the same way, perfect physical health is pursued to extremes and assumes a kind of mythical status, to be sought in every imaginable way, leading to anxiety in the attempt to control every symptom. Thus emerges the thirst for things like Steiner schooling, homeopathic treatments, organic food, organic cotton, natural remedies, afternoon outings in the car in search of noncontaminated produce, and all the rest, leading to disapproving glances being cast toward "conventional" moms whose kids take antibiotics.

We need to give our kids a break, even when we struggle to understand them fully. Their teachers can't understand them and neither can we. They are a generation forced to undergo an infinite variety of stimuli—too many to be able to sort through them all—and who therefore find themselves unable to cope with all that is laid before them. They don't have the time to do so. Their tasks are legion, and the stress is overwhelming. They have too little time to consolidate things. Let's be merciful to them then, and let's be merciful to ourselves, too, for we are, in many ways, pioneer parents.

Three Years Later . . .

If truth be told, the letter to Marta was really aimed at me. Marta is someone you ask advice from, you don't give it! So the question "How did it all turn out?" should really concern my children and not hers. It's just a pity I find myself asking that question on the same day I had to call in a decontamination team to open a path through the mountain of junk in the boys' bedroom. My usual reprimand is a typical, gentle exaggeration I often use: "When I was a girl, I used to fetch water with pitchers and balance them on my head to bring them back to the house." In response to such a statement, the two boys are inclined to look at each other and say, "What do you think? Why does dad live with this woman and not with a nicer and younger wife?"

However, for the record, Marta's three children are all doing very well and are the living incarnation of how I would like my own to turn out: polite, quiet, obedient, kind, and admirable. I hope that within their four walls, they occasionally do something wrong; otherwise, the comparison (I know you are not supposed to compare kids, but doing so is moms' favorite sport) would be truly demoralizing for me.

Yet—and I owe this gem of wisdom to Marta—we always think that other people's children are better than our own, that they have all the gifts we would like for our kids. That's pretty normal. You teach them as best you can and you acknowledge that whatever is lacking in them you've not been able to transmit. No one can teach their kids everything. How could I have ever brought up kids to be sensible, steady, and well-balanced when I am as mad as a hatter—or as they say in Italian, "as mad as a giraffe," which is perhaps a better analogy because I am a giraffe who married a bear. What can you expect from that pairing?

How could we ever have had reserved, quiet children when we couldn't even convince the taxi driver on the night of our wedding that we were genuinely just married? (I went to the movies still wearing my veil!) On the other hand, there are some things—in fact, many things—that my children will learn in other ways from other people. (Maybe they'll be blessed with a little school friend who will understand chemistry, like the little girl who used to sit next to me in class? Such are the quirks of fate.)

So I have come to the conclusion that the main challenge of our life as parents, and mine as a mother, lies precisely in this: We have to learn to give them their freedom. We need to move beyond the stage of complete fusion with the little pink bundle of love who is totally dependent on you and on whom you project all your hopes and dreams. At that stage no one will contradict you if you happen to think your child is the new Tolstoy simply because she managed to compose the word *PINO* with toy letters. The challenge comes when they move beyond that stage, when our children begin to take a healthy distance from us; when they are no longer little satellites revolving around us; and when they grow up, not always in the way we would like. The point is this: It's not for us to choose how their life will pan out. We have to get used to running the risk that they won't turn out the way we had planned (what an ugly word to use in relation to bringing up children) but that they may actually be better than we had "planned."

We have to have patience, let time pass, learn to accept things, and acknowledge that, on occasion, times will be tough; they might be dirty, naughty, and much more, but they will always be our children.

Don Luigi Giussani, the founder of the Communion and Liberation Movement, always said that a child's adolescence was the greatest test for a couple. So be it . . . if we have to go down into the trenches, down into the trenches we will go. (Memo to self: Don't forget the eight-hour sun block for periods of bad weather or the Diet Coke for the all-night assignments. And remember lots of air sanitizer—adolescent bedrooms tend to stink. Tennis shoes, even when they have been sanitized, still give off a foul reek.) We'll get used to the fact that we will be considered ancient like the Pooh (an Italian pop band from the 1960s) and as useless as a newspaper made of . . . well . . . paper! They get their news via some sort of app. Can you imagine it? But we won't be defeated.

I still chuckle at the memory of the conversation between my son and his friend:

"What year was the fire that burned the Shroud of Turin?"

"I'm not sure. Let's ask your mom."

"Come on, she's ancient. She must have been about forty at that time."

We will be criticized, but we won't break down, because the respect that we try to show for each other will be far more powerful and eloquent than 1,000 sermons. We will know how to smile when the storm blows all around us, because we Christians live like characters in an American film that always has a happy ending. If our heart is at peace with God, then we lay all our cares on Him in complete trust.

We'll remind each other, even in the eye of the storm, to skip, to laugh, to take a cake to our neighbor, to sing in the shower, to go and see *The Big Lebowski*, to wear bottle-green high heels, and to spray on a bit of perfume before going to bed, because despite it all, the storm will pass.

Acknowledgments

Since I will probably never write anything again that might be worthy of publication, unless a new market opens up for useful post-it notes, notes for the new teacher (you need a particular skill to write a letter to someone when you can't remember his or her name), or shopping lists for husbands (this is also an art form that requires you to place the most important things at the top so that they don't get crossed out and forgotten), I thought I should probably acknowledge here some of the debts of gratitude I owe. This way I also avoid a whole lot of phone calls, some of which, such as the one that would be required to Saint Therese of Lisieux, could be a bit technically complex.

Thanks be to God for all those things I know I must thank Him for and also those that I don't even pretend to understand. Since we make it into Paradise on recommendation rather than merit, Our Lady, please put in a good word for us!

Thanks to the two popes of my life who reassure us that our beliefs are not fruits of our own imagination. To St. John Paul, who spoke definitive words about women and about life. To the great Benedict XVI, who bore for us a media martyrdom without precedent.

Thanks to the Church, of which I am proud to be part, which over the centuries has produced some of the finest minds in human history: Thomas Aquinas, Augustine, Bernard, Theresa of Avila, Catherine of Sienna, Therese of Lisieux, and thousands of other known and unknown.

Coming back down to earth, thanks first and foremost to my husband Guido for his constant love and support and, despite everything, his dedication, generosity, patience, ability to solve problems, and sense of humor.

Thanks to our four lovely children, Tommaso, Bernardo, Livia, and Lavinia just for existing, just for being the way they are and for putting up with me being rather more tired and distracted than usual for a few months during the writing of this book. Thanks too for not breaking even a single arm despite my reduced vigilance!

Thanks to my parents, Nicola and Rosella, for having said yes to life for me and for having brought me up, all in all, as a decent person. Thanks too for all the lovely little necklaces (and everything else) that they have given to me as gifts. Thanks too to my brother Giovanni and sister Chiara, who always answer my calls and never hang up.

Thanks to my spiritual parents: Father Emidio, whose wisdom I have shamelessly sought out, and Father Bernardo, Sister Chiara Serena, Mother Elvira, Antonella T., and Don Ignazio, who have nourished and supported me in my faith.

Thanks to my husband's parents, Livio and Marisa, who said yes to life for him and looked after him until they could land him on me. Thanks especially for all the help with nursery rhymes and trays of lasagna (and thanks to Raffaella, who is head of the sweet department).

Thanks to all my female friends who are a constant source of comfort and discussion. To Marina, who took an active role in the writing of this book, giving me her intelligence, her sensitivity, and her notes. To Daniela, who is my personal moral theologian on-call 24 hours a day. To Alessandra, Angela, Antonella, Carmen, Chiara B., Chiara M., Claudia, Costanza, Cristiana, Elisabetta, Emanuela, Francesca F., Francesca M., Giorgia, Isa, Lucia, Maria Cristina, Maria Grazia, Maura, Morena, Noemi, Paola, Patrizia, Rita, Roberta, Silvia, Silvana, and Stefania: They are treasured friends and constant inspirations. In this book, there's a little bit of each of them (and also of Ilda and Paola, who sadly are no longer with us).

Thanks to Paolo, my dear friend and indispensable master of humor, to Giancarlo, who didn't let on that he noticed my heavy eyes as I watched the screens in the newsroom after too many late nights spent writing, and to Gabriele, who has always been so important to me at the crucial moments of my life.

Thanks to all who are on the side of life, however they show it—to Carlo Casini and all the others. Thanks to Giuliano Ferrara, who has made the cause of life glamorous.

Thanks to Jean Kerr and Erma Bombeck, whose books made me cry with laughter during the children's midnight feeds. (During the day, to make a good impression, it's better to read some elegant classic published by Adelphi or Fondazione Lorenzo Valla.) Thanks to Jo Croissant, whose *Il mistero della donna*, from which I drew much inspiration, helped me and many of my friends understand the mysterious and marvelous nature of the mission entrusted to us.

Thanks to Sonzogno Publishers, who welcomed me with open arms. In particular, a word of gratitude to my editor Patricia Chendi, who I wish I could borrow as my personal motivator at home, every morning as I prepare to take on the challenges of the day. To Luca and Cesare De Michelis, who trusted me and to Francesca Prevedello, who was always there to listen to me as though I was a lucid and rational human being.

A special thanks to Camillo Langone, who inspired me and accompanied me. Without him, not one line of this book would have been written. That may not have been a great loss to humanity, but thanks anyway, Camillo.

 TAN·BOOKS

TAN Books is the Publisher You Can Trust With Your Faith.

TAN Books was founded in 1967 to preserve the spiritual, intellectual, and liturgical traditions of the Catholic Church. At a critical moment in history TAN kept alive the great classics of the Faith and drew many to the Church. In 2008 TAN was acquired by Saint Benedict Press. Today TAN continues to teach and defend the Faith to a new generation of readers.

TAN publishes more than 600 booklets, Bibles, and books. Popular subject areas include theology and doctrine, prayer and the supernatural, history, biography, and the lives of the saints. TAN's line of educational and homeschooling resources is featured at TANHomeschool.com.

TAN publishes under several imprints, including TAN, Neumann Press, ACS Books, and the Confraternity of the Precious Blood. Sister imprints include Saint Benedict Press, Catholic Courses, and Catholic Scripture Study International.

For more information about TAN,
or to request a free catalog, visit
TANBooks.com

Or call us toll-free at
(800) 437-5876

Ryan and Mary-Rose Verret

Witness to Love

How to Help the Next Generation Build
Marriages That Survive and Thrive

Good Marriages Don't Happen by Accident

Ryan and Mary-Rose Verret

"In this ground-breaking book, the Verrets share hard-won insights with those willing to become a source of light and comfort to couples considering marriage or just starting out."

—Art and Laraine Bennett
Authors of *The Temperament God Gave You*
(Sophia Institute Press 2005)

Today as never before threats to marriage loom. To overcome them young couples need good hearts and God's grace.

And each of these couples needs a "Witness to Love." They need generous, seasoned husbands and wives who are willing to mentor them—and show them marriage as God meant it to be.

In Witness to Love, Mary-Rose and Ryan Verret issue an urgent call to help turn the tide of broken families. They give married couples the tools to encourage young couples in desperate need of mentors. And they issue a challenge to us all: Share your lives, share your heart, share your love. Make disciples!

Ryan and Mary-Rose Verret are the founders of Witness to Love, a not-for-profit marriage preparation renewal ministry.

978-1-61890-698-4 • *Paperbound*

Spread the Faith with . . .

TAN·BOOKS

A Division of Saint Benedict Press, LLC

TAN books are powerful tools for evangelization. They lift the mind to God and change lives. Millions of readers have found in TAN books and booklets an effective way to teach and defend the Faith, soften hearts, and grow in prayer and holiness of life.

Throughout history the faithful have distributed Catholic literature and sacramentals to save souls. St. Francis de Sales passed out his own pamphlets to win back those who had abandoned the Faith. Countless others have distributed the Miraculous Medal to prompt conversions and inspire deeper devotion to God. Our customers use TAN books in that same spirit.

If you have been helped by this or another TAN title, share it with others. Become a TAN Missionary and share our life changing books and booklets with your family, friends and community. We'll help by providing special discounts for books and booklets purchased in quantity for purposes of evangelization. Write or call us for additional details.

TAN Books
Attn: TAN Missionaries Department
PO Box 410487
Charlotte, NC 28241

Toll-free (800) 437-5876
missionaries@TANBooks.com